The New Zealand Fish and Shellfish Cookbook

Heather Currie • Susan Marris • Jennifer Brasted

New Zealand Fishing Industry Board

WHITCOULLS PUBLISHERS
Christchurch   London

Front cover photo: A selection of New Zealand fish and shellfish (*Sal Criscillo*)

First published 1986
©1986 New Zealand Fishing Industry Board

Whitcoulls Publishers
Christchurch, New Zealand

All rights reserved. No part of this publication may be reproduced, stored in a retrieval system, or transmitted in any form or by any means, electronic, mechanical, photocopying, recording or otherwise, without prior written permission of the publishers.

ISBN 0 7233 0776 8

Typeset by Saba Graphics Ltd, Christchurch
Printed by Kok Wah Press (Pte) Ltd, Singapore

CONTENTS

Introduction	4
Main New Zealand Species	6
Nutrition Facts	8
Hints for Perfectly Prepared Seafood	12
Cooking Characteristics	13
Storage Life of Seafood	19
Fish	22
Frozen Fish	30
Whole Fish	32
Smoked Seafood	33
Shellfish	34
Crabs	39
Prawns and Shrimps	41
Rock Lobster (Crayfish)	41
Squid	44
Sashimi	46
Microwave Magic	47
Weights and Measures	50
Hors-d'oeuvre	51
Soups	60
Starters and Entrées	70
Light Meals	80
Main Courses	90
Salads	120
Barbecues	130
Sauces	139
Garnishes	146
Index	150

INTRODUCTION

Despite having a long association with the sea through Maori mythology, European migration and recreational activity, New Zealanders have not been great fish eaters. This is common to many countries that have a strong pastoral farming tradition with ample supplies of red meat available. Australia, Argentina and the USA all have similar fish consumption levels to New Zealand.

Since the New Zealand Fishing Industry Board was established in 1964, one of its major tasks has been to stimulate greater interest in seafood among New Zealand consumers. This has been done by extensive work in schools, seminars for teachers, chefs and catering institutions, recipe leaflets and booklets for the public, cooking demonstrations and major promotions such as 'Fish the Family Dish' and 'Fish for a Compliment'.

The last ten years have seen the benefits of this work. There has been a considerable increase in the awareness of seafood which initially stopped a slow decline in consumption and, in the last five years, has resulted in a steady growth in the seafood consumed per capita in this country. This increase came about initially through the restaurant sector, with the greater variety and excellence of the seafood offered, and more recently with the wider range and higher quality of product available in improved retail outlets and supermarkets with an updated image.

As a result of these trends, consumers are willing to experience all the exciting products available from the sea and are eager to try many seafoods they would not have considered some years ago.

There is now without doubt a need for a comprehensive seafood cookbook which does justice to the wonderful range of seafood available from New Zealand waters.

We believe this book achieves this, and have been pleased to be associated with Whitcoulls Publishers in its publication.

N.E. Jarman
General Manager
New Zealand Fishing Industry Board

SEAFOOD LANDINGS AT PRINCIPAL NEW ZEALAND PORTS

Tasman Sea

- **Mangonui:** Snapper, Groper, Mullet, Rock Lobster, Tarakihi
- **Whangarei:** Trevally, John Dory, Eel, Snapper, Leatherjacket, Rock Lobster
- **Auckland/Manukau:** Snapper, John Dory, Flounder, Rock Oysters, Squid, Mussels, Eel
- **Mercury Bay:** Snapper, Trevally, Scallops, Gemfish, Rock Lobster, Tarakihi
- **Thames:** Snapper, Trevally, Flounder, Scallops
- **Tauranga:** Snapper, Trevally, Tarakihi, Skipjack, Mackerel
- **New Plymouth:** Snapper, Trevally, Kahawai, Gurnard
- **Gisborne:** Tarakihi, Mackerel, Silver Kingfish, Rock Lobster, Skipjack, Tuna, Hoki, Groper
- **Wanganui:** Shark, Leatherjacket, Mackerel, Squid, Snapper, Gurnard
- **Napier:** Trevally, Silver Kingfish, John Dory, Sole, Rock Lobster, Snapper, Tarakihi, Gurnard
- **Motueka:** Snapper, Barracouta, Flounder, Scallops, Hoki, Orange Roughy, Hake
- **Nelson:** Warehou, Hake, John Dory, Squid, Leatherjacket, Mussels, Oysters, Scallops, Hoki, Orange Roughy
- **Wellington:** Tarakihi, Groper, Ling, Hoki, Rock Lobster
- **Westport:** Sole, Red Cod, Gurnard
- **Greymouth:** Albacore Tuna, Red Cod, Sole, Hoki, Hake, Brill, Turbot
- **Kaikoura:** Shark, Moki, Ling, Kahawai
- **Lyttelton:** Tarakihi, Gurnard, Elephant Fish, Eel
- **Akaroa:** Gurnard, Elephant Fish, Red Cod
- **Timaru:** Gurnard, Elephant Fish, Tarakihi, Orange Roughy, Squid
- **Port Chalmers:** Sole, Tarakihi, Flounder, Rock Lobster, Orange Roughy
- **Bluff:** Blue Cod, Monkfish, Rock Lobster, Oysters
- **Stewart Island:** Blue Cod, Rock Lobster

Chatham Islands: Blue Cod, Tarakihi, Rock Lobster

South Pacific Ocean

- 0-500 metres
- Deeper than 500 metres

MAIN NEW ZEALAND SPECIES

Trevally

Red Cod

Blue Cod

Sand Flounder

Grey Mullet

Groper

Jack Mackerels

Blue Moki

Leatherjacket

Rig

Kahawai

Orange Roughy

John Dory

Butterfish

Gurnard

Monkfish

New Zealand Sole

Skipjack Tuna

Ling

Hoki

Blue Warehou

Black Oreo Dory

Hake

Barracouta

Snapper

Tarakihi

Gemfish

Northern Kingfish

NUTRITION FACTS

In selecting what they eat, people are becoming more conscious of the need to choose food that is both nutritious and non-fattening.

Good nutrition is the key to good health. A balanced diet is therefore essential, as no one food contains all the required nutrients.

Fish and shellfish have historically been recognised as a source of essential nutrients. They play an important part in establishing and maintaining a healthy diet and consumers are increasingly aware of the benefits of utilising the delicious range of seafoods now available.

Seafood consumption in New Zealand is therefore rising steadily. In fact, during the period from the late 1970s to the mid 1980s, New Zealanders doubled their consumption of fish to over 20 kg per person per year (this is calculated in terms of whole fish and doesn't include shellfish). Much of this increase is the result of the growth of the restaurant trade, but New Zealanders are also changing from red to white meats when buying for home-cooked meals — and these 'white meats' include seafoods.

Seafood has attained, therefore, even more prominence recently in the diets of the health- and nutrition-conscious. As medical research has discovered more information about the benefits of less fat and cholesterol in the diet, so too has come increasing evidence of the positive attributes of a high seafood diet, as opposed to a high red meat one.

Many medical researchers believe that the high incidence of particular forms of cancer in New Zealand, such as bowel and breast cancer, is due in part to the consumption of too much animal protein. When consumed, this animal protein often has associated with it high amounts of cholesterol and hard or saturated animal fats.

In contrast, extensive research over recent years into the properties of fish fat has revealed that the fat of fish lowers cholesterol levels, prevents hardening of the arteries and may assist in reducing the incidence of breast cancer.

A Danish doctor, Dr Dyerberg, has studied the eating habits of the Eskimos, who consume large quantities of seal and fish. He found that the blood of Eskimos contains large quantities of eicosapentaenoic acid (EPA) which has been shown to be effective in the prevention of heart disease.

The EPA found in fish is more effective in cutting down cholesterol levels in the body than the linoleic acid in vegetable oil because it is highly unsaturated. EPA also controls blood coagulation and is effective in reducing the possibility of blood clots. For these reasons, fish fat must be considered differently from animal fat of beef or pork origin.

The oil content in New Zealand fish varies between species, ranging from 1 percent to 15 percent, and averaging 4 percent. Darker species such as tuna, kahawai and mackerel are high in oil, and some fish with white flesh, such as tarakihi, have a relatively high oil content. In general, however, the whiter the flesh the less fat it contains.

The amount of oil in seafood is relatively low when compared with many cuts of meat. Furthermore, these fats and oils are mainly unsaturated or polyunsaturated, a major advantage over red or white meats.

It must always be remembered that the method of cooking fish will affect the level of fat in the prepared fish dish — deep-fried fish, for instance, has a much higher fat content than grilled fish. It is only the omega-3 fatty acids in the fish which are beneficial to health, as opposed to the omega-6 fatty acids in the vegetable oil or the saturated animal fats in which the fish would be fried.

Finfish contains no measurable carbohydrate but shellfish such as oysters, scallops, mussels and squid contain small amounts of carbohydrate in the form of glycogen. Carbohydrate is utilised in the body for energy.

Seafood contains phosphorus, fluoride, magnesium, iodine, calcium, sodium and potassium. Where fish bones are eaten, as in canned fish, the amount of available calcium is increased.

Many seafoods provide a useful source of trace elements such as iron, zinc, copper and selenium.

Seafood is a good source of the B-group vitamins, especially thiamin, riboflavin and niacin, and it contains traces of vitamins C and K. The liver of fish is a good source of vitamins A and D (cod liver oil).

Energy Value and Protein

Comparison of energy value and protein content of some commonly eaten protein foods (per 100 g serving raw edible portion).

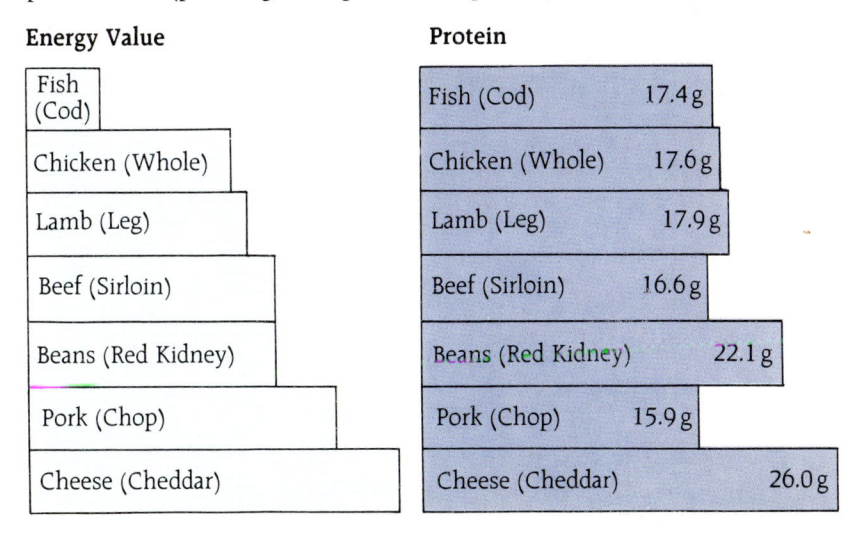

Energy Value

| Fish (Cod) |
| Chicken (Whole) |
| Lamb (Leg) |
| Beef (Sirloin) |
| Beans (Red Kidney) |
| Pork (Chop) |
| Cheese (Cheddar) |

Protein

Fish (Cod)	17.4 g
Chicken (Whole)	17.6 g
Lamb (Leg)	17.9 g
Beef (Sirloin)	16.6 g
Beans (Red Kidney)	22.1 g
Pork (Chop)	15.9 g
Cheese (Cheddar)	26.0 g

As the above chart illustrates, a 100-g serving of fish is low in calories but high in protein, compared with other foods commonly included in the diet.

Basic Nutritional Composition of Fish

Nutritional analysis of finfish species commercially available in New Zealand, showing composition (g) and calculated gross energy per 100 g net weight of fillet.

	Crude Protein	Oil	Moisture	Ash	Kcal	Kjoule
Alfonsino	16.9	14.0	68.3	0.8	218	913
Albacore Tuna	26.4	4.7	67.5	1.4	181	758
Barracouta	21.3	3.1	74.2	1.4	140	584
Baxters Dogfish	17.5	1.0	80.6	1.0	100	420
Black Oreo Dory*	17.6	5.3	76.0	1.1	71	299
Black Slickhead	9.9	0.6	88.3	1.1	57	239
Blue Cod	18.1	0.8	79.9	1.3	102	425
Blue Moki	20.8	1.6	76.3	1.3	123	515
Blue Mackerel	22.3	10.0	66.3	1.4	209	875
Cardinal Fish	18.7	1.7	78.6	1.0	113	473
Common Warehou	20.8	4.4	73.5	1.3	149	624
Elephant Fish	22.5	1.0	75.3	1.2	126	529
Frostfish	19.5	1.1	78.4	1.1	112	467
Gemfish	19.9	2.8	76.3	1.0	130	542
Giant Stargazer	18.2	0.6	80.2	1.0	100	419
Grenadiers (Rattail sp.)	18.3	0.5	80.3	0.9	100	418
Grey Mullet	21.3	1.3	76.3	1.1	123	514
Hake	16.4	1.6	81.0	1.1	100	419
Hapuku (Groper)	19.7	1.8	77.0	1.5	119	499
Hoki	14.6	0.8	83.7	1.0	89	371
Jack Mackerel (T. declivis)	19.8	7.0	71.9	1.3	168	704
Jack Mackerel (T. Novaezelandia)	20.9	3.3	74.4	1.4	139	584
Javelin Fish (Grenadier)	16.7	0.8	81.7	0.8	94	394
John Dory	20.6	0.8	77.5	1.1	209	874
Kahawai	22.6	6.4	70.0	1.0	177	741
Kingfish	21.4	1.2	76.3	1.2	123	513
Leatherjacket	18.6	0.8	79.7	0.9	104	436
Lemon Sole	17.9	1.5	79.6	1.0	107	448
Ling	19.9	0.8	78.3	1.0	111	464
Lookdown Dory	17.9	2.5	78.9	0.7	122	509
New Zealand Sole	19.4	1.2	78.4	1.1	112	469
Orange Roughy*	14.7	8.5	75.9	0.9	66	278
Parore	19.3	1.2	78.3	1.2	112	467
Pale Ghost Shark	17.4	1.1	80.2	1.3	101	422
Pilchards (H&G)	20.8	4.1	73.3	1.8	146	612
Piper	20.6	1.2	76.6	1.6	118	495
Porae	20.8	3.6	74.5	1.0	142	592
Rays Bream	21.0	1.5	75.6	1.9	123	516
Red Cod	17.2	0.7	80.8	1.3	96	401
Red Gurnard	19.8	0.9	78.1	1.1	111	466

*Although the oil content in these species is high, much of this oil is in wax ester form, unavailable to the human body. Therefore, the kilocalorie or kilojoule levels remain low.

Ribaldo	17.9	0.5	80.5	0.9	98	409
Ridge-scaled Rattail	17.4	0.6	81.2	0.9	96	402
Rig	21.4	0.9	76.7	1.1	120	501
Rudder Fish	14.1	18.1	67.0	0.8	242	1011
Salmon (fresh water)	19.7	2.9	75.8	1.6	129	542
Salmon (sea pen)	19.2	7.2	72.4	1.3	167	698
Sand Flounder	17.3	0.8	80.8	1.1	97	408
School Shark	21.2	1.0	76.4	1.4	120	500
Sea Perch	15.8	0.6	82.8	0.9	88	368
Silver Dory	17.3	1.2	80.6	0.9	101	424
Silver Warehou	18.5	11.0	68.9	1.6	199	831
Skipjack Tuna	25.6	8.2	64.7	1.5	209	877
Slender Tuna	19.8	24.1	54.7	1.4	327	1369
Smooth Oreo Dory*	11.2	3.6	84.2	1.0	49	208
Snapper	19.4	1.6	77.7	1.3	116	485
Southern Blue Whiting	15.9	0.7	82.5	0.9	89	373
Spiny Dogfish	18.8	5.2	74.9	1.1	146	612
Swollenhead Conger Eel	17.6	2.8	78.2	1.4	118	492
Tarakihi	20.5	2.9	75.4	1.2	134	559
Trevally	20.4	2.7	76.0	0.9	131	549
White Warehou	15.1	12.1	71.5	1.3	191	800
Yellow Belly Flounder	18.9	1.2	78.7	1.2	110	458
Yellow-eyed Mullet	18.8	1.7	78.5	1.0	114	476

Basic Nutritional Composition of Shellfish and Crustacea

Nutritional analysis of shellfish and crustacea commercially available in New Zealand, showing composition of edible parts (g) and calculated gross energy per 100 g net weight of edible material.

	Crude Protein	Oil	Moisture	Ash	Soluble Carbohydrate	Kcal	Kjoule
Arrow Squid	19.2	1.7	77.5	1.4	0.2	116	487
Bluff Oyster	16.0	3.0	79.4	1.6	3.1	123	516
Broad Squid	19.1	1.9	77.9	1.4	0.1	117	491
Cockle	8.2	0.9	87.8	2.5	0.6	54	224
Green Mussel	11.9	2.1	80.9	1.7	3.4	95	398
Horse Mussel	14.8	0.5	81.0	1.3	2.4	91	382
Kina	10.8	5.4	80.9	2.3	0.6	108	455
Pacific Oyster	13.1	3.2	79.7	2.7	1.3	103	432
Paddle Crab	15.5	0.9	80.9	1.3	0.9	93	388
Paua	21.7	1.0	75.7	1.6	0.9	126	526
Pipi	8.2	0.7	87.0	3.6	0.5	51	214
Rock Lobster (Crayfish)	21.9	0.8	75.0	1.7	0.7	124	519
Scallop	15.4	1.3	86.6	1.9	2.7	103	432
Tuatua	16.7	2.2	72.0	2.9	6.2	132	553
Warty Squid	14.1	1.3	83.2	1.2	0.2	86	361

HINTS FOR PERFECTLY PREPARED SEAFOOD

How to Test if Seafood is Cooked
Fresh fish and shellfish have a glossy and translucent appearance prior to cooking. To test that seafood is cooked, insert the pointed end of a knife and check that the flesh at the thickest part of the whole fish, fillet, steak or shellfish has turned opaque. The flesh should have lost its glossiness and it should flake more easily than when in its raw state.

Herbs to Use with Seafood
The golden rule is that as long as the flavour or quantity of the herb does not overpower the seafood, many herbs may be used, either individually or combined.

The following impart a delicious flavour:

	Seafood Cocktails	Salads	Tomato-based Dishes	Milk-based Dishes	Stuffings	Marinades	Poaching Liquids	OTHER SUGGESTIONS
ALLSPICE				•	•	•		Pickling brine.
BASIL	•	•	•	•	•			Use with crab, shrimp, mackerel, salmon and tuna.
BAY LEAF			•	•		•	•	Pickling brine.
CHERVIL			•	•	•	•		Garnishes, dips, tartare sauce.
CHIVES	•	•		•				Garnishes, dips, sauces.
CURRY		•	•	•		•		Casseroles, sandwich fillings, dips, sauces, curry butter for grilled fillets.
DILL	•	•	•	•	•	•		Dips, spreads, salmon or sole.
FENNEL		•	•				•	Classic bouillabaisse, fennel butter for grilled fish.
GARLIC	•		•			•		Lemon garlic butter, sauces for grilled fish, recipes for squid and mussels.
GINGER		•		•			•	Chinese-style stir-fry dishes, fruit sauces for deep-fried fish and shellfish.
MUSTARD	•	•				•		Sauces for basting grilled and barbecued fish and dipping deep-fried seafood.
NUTMEG				•				Seafood Newburg, fish croquettes, pickling liquid.
PAPRIKA		•	•	•	•			Garnishes, croquettes, coatings for fried fish.
PARSLEY	•	•	•	•	•	•		Flavouring or garnish for almost any fish or shellfish dish.
ROSEMARY			•	•	•			Grilled steaks or fillets.
SAGE				•	•			Baked or grilled steaks or fillets.
SAVOURY		•	•	•				Fish stews, grilled fish, recipes for sole, crab or shrimp.
TARRAGON	•	•	•		•		•	Spreads, grilled fish, recipes for salmon, sole, shrimp and crab.
THYME	•		•	•	•		•	Classic bouillabaisse, spreads.

To Keep Grilled Seafood Moist
Pour 1-2 cm water into the grill pan. Place the seafood on the grill rack over the water.

Under the heat of the grill a little of the water evaporates, keeping the seafood moist. This method also makes the pan very easy to clean as juices or toppings don't burn onto the pan.

To Clean Hands
After handling fish, first wash your hands and scrub your nails in cold water to rinse off the fish juices and prevent them 'cooking'. Then wash your hands thoroughly with warm, soapy water.

Remember to follow the same procedure with your chopping board, especially if it is a wooden one.

COOKING CHARACTERISTICS

Substitution
If, when you visit your local seafood retailer, you find that he hasn't got the family's favourite fish in stock, don't leave empty-handed.

Very few recipes require a specific species to make them a success. This means that there are many varieties, often cheaper and more readily available, which can be substituted. With over 70 different seafoods commercially available in New Zealand, you should be able to get something to suit your planned recipe.

Ask your seafood retailer for assistance when choosing fish, but if in doubt, take this book with you when shopping for seafood and use it as a guide. The Cooking Characteristics Chart' on page 15 has been compiled to assist you to choose a substitute fish if your favourite variety is unavailable or proves to be outside your grocery budget for the week.

If you use this chart as a guide to buying seafood, you will get the right fish for the right recipe. No longer should you end up with a casserole full of flaked fish instead of nice chunks if you correctly choose a firm-textured fish rather than a delicate-textured one. The family budget may also be helped by your being able to buy lesser-known species at a lower price because you know what to use them for!

Cooking Characteristics Chart
The seafoods listed in the following chart are commercially caught species. The terms used in the chart are explained here in more detail.

Texture
For cooking purposes, fish are divided into categories of texture, depending on how the fillet reacts when cooked. It is most important to select the correct fish for the chosen recipe.

Delicate-textured fish flakes easily when cooked. It is ideal for dishes requiring either little handling or flaked fish.

Delicate-textured fish is best baked, foil-baked or microwaved. It should be well coated before frying.

Medium-textured fish is multi-purpose, suitable for all cooking methods. Although most will flake into thick flakes they will hold their shape well during cooking.

Medium-textured fish is best soused, marinated, microwaved or poached.

Firm-textured fish will not flake readily when cooked, so it is ideal for dishes where the fish must retain its shape.

Firm-textured fish is best in casseroles, soups, stir-fries and when steamed or poached — any method using a moist heat.

Oil Content

Generally, all fish have a relatively low oil content in comparison to lamb, beef and dairy products.

But the oil content of a fish should be considered when selecting the method of cooking. As frying increases the oil level, species with a high oil content should preferably be cooked by other methods.

Colour When Cooked

This is very important in commercial cooking. It is difficult to tell what colour raw fish will be when it's cooked, so for this information refer to the following chart.

Flavour

Although some dishes traditionally require a delicately flavoured white fish, there are other dishes which use a fuller flavoured fish. These fish are often more economical and may have advantages over the traditional delicate species.

The flavour of the fish being used is important as it determines the cooking method, the type of sauce and accompaniments — all of which must ensure that the flavour of the seafood is enhanced and not masked.

Special Features

Points of interest not covered under the other headings are noted in this section.

Species	Texture and Oil Content*	Colour When Cooked	Flavour	Special Features
Alfonsino	Firm, High oil content	White	Medium	Skin attractive scarlet-orange.
Anchovy	Medium, High oil content	Dark	Strong	Usually canned but can be eaten fresh.
Barracouta	Medium, Medium oil content	Dark flesh, whitens when cooked	Medium	Suitable for smoking. Difficult to fillet due to an irregular bone structure. Often smoked and/or canned.
Bluenose (Bonita, Blue Bream, Stoneye)	Firm, succulent, Medium oil content	Whitens on cooking	Medium	
Brill	Delicate, moist, Medium oil content	Apricot flesh, whitens when cooked	Delicate	
Butterfish (Greenbone)	Medium, succulent, Medium oil content	White	Sweet, delicate	
Blue Cod	Medium, Low oil content	Pink flesh, whitens on cooking	Delicate	Often smoked.
Red Cod	Delicate, moist, Low oil content	White	Sweet, medium	Flakes readily, often smoked.
John Dory	Medium, Low oil content	White	Delicate	Fillets easily boned.
Frostfish (Cutlassfish, Ribbon Fish)	Delicate, Low oil content	White	Delicate	Similar to hoki, but more delicate.
Garfish (Piper, Halfbeak)	Medium, Medium oil content	White	Medium	Remove gut, then bone by placing cut side on board and rolling the fish with a bottle along spine. Pull bone off flesh.
Gemfish	Delicate, easily flaked, Low oil content	White	Medium	Ideal smoked.
Grenadiers (Rattails, Macrourids)	Delicate, Low oil content	White	Medium	Flesh of some species similar to red cod.
Lookdown Dory	Medium, Medium oil content	White	Delicate	Fillets small.
Conger Eel	Firm, High oil content	White	Less oily than freshwater eels	Does not flake readily on cooking.
Shortfinned Eel Longfinned Eel	Firm, Medium oil content	White	Delicate	Excellent texture and delicate flavour when smoked.
Sand Flounder (Dab), Yellowbelly Flounder	Delicate, Low oil content	White	Delicate	
Groper (Hapuku)	Firm, Low oil content	White	Medium	Makes good steak. Has excellent roes—large and suitable for smoking.

*Oil content classification: Low 0%-3%, Medium 3.1%-6%, High 6.1% upwards

Species	Texture and Oil Content	Colour When Cooked	Flavour	Special Features
Red Gurnard	Medium, succulent Low oil content	White	Sweet, medium	Low fat content. Scales too small to need removing.
Hake	Delicate Low oil content	White	Delicate	Few bones. Large, moist fillets.
Hoki	Delicate, succulent Low oil content	White	Delicate	Flakes easily. Fillets ideal for portion control, no pin bones. Often bought skinless, boneless and individually frozen.
Kahawai	Medium High oil content	Dark, lightens on cooking	Strong flavour	Moist heat method of cooking, good soused or smoked.
Northern Kingfish	Firm, succulent Low oil content	Dark, lightens on cooking	Medium	Often sold as steaks or may be cooked whole. Popular substitute for groper steaks.
Leatherjacket (Creamfish)	Delicate Low oil content	Cream	Similar to flounder	Usually sold headed, gutted and skinned. Average-sized fish provides entrée-sized servings (2 for main course). Highly underrated by NZ chefs, large export market to Australia.
Ling	Very firm Low oil content	Very white contrasts well with ingredients such as tomato, curry, and mushrooms	Medium	Excellent smoked product. Holds shape well on cooking.
Blue Mackerel	Medium High oil content	Dark, lightens on cooking	Meaty	High fat content. Excellent canned. Small fish ideal served whole. Good steaked.
Jack Mackerel	Medium High oil content	Dark, lightens on cooking	Meaty	Suitable for canning and smoking. Distinguished from Blue Mackerel by extra pin bones at tail. Good steaked.
Blue Moki	Medium, moist Low oil content	Greyish-white when cooked	Medium	Ideal for chowders.
Monkfish (Rock Cod or Stargazer)	Firm texture, not readily flaked Low oil content	Pearly white flesh	Similar to rock lobster in flavour and texture	A succulent, underrated and under-utilised species. Best purchased filleted due to irregular bone structure. Check flesh for pin bones. Ideal marinated.
Black Oreo Dory	Dense, not readily flaked Medium oil content	White	Good flavour	Fillets small.
Smooth Oreo Dory	Dense, not readily flaked Medium oil content	Very white	Good flavour	Fillets larger and more moist than Black Dory and could be tried as a substitute for Orange Roughy.
Sea Perch (Scarpee)	Medium Low oil content	White	Medium	Succulent. Ideal cooked whole, has attractive colour and shape. One fish per main course.
Pilchard (Sardine)	Medium, firm Medium oil content	Dark	Medium	Suitable for canning or cooking whole.

Species	Texture and Oil Content	Colour When Cooked	Flavour	Special Features
Ribaldo (Deep Sea Cod)	Medium, firm Medium oil content	White	Medium	
Orange Roughy (Deep Sea Perch)	Medium texture, coarse flakes High oil content	Pearly white	Delicate shellfish flavour	Requires deep skinning to remove subcutaneous fat layer. Able to be cooked by any method.
Quinnat Salmon	Firm High oil content	Pink	Very delicate	Farmed, often smoked.
Snapper	Medium coarse flakes Low oil content	White	Medium	Excellent cooked whole.
Lemon Sole	Delicate, moist Low oil content	White or whitens on cooking	Sweet delicate flavour	Upper fillets slightly darker.
New Zealand Sole	Delicate, moist Low oil content	White or whitens on cooking	Sweet delicate flavour	Upper fillets slightly darker.
Sprat (New Zealand Herring)	Medium High oil content	Darkish	Medium to strong	Suitable for canning.
Tarakihi	Medium, moist Low to medium oil content	White	Medium	Excellent cooked whole. Flesh retains shape better than snapper.
Trevally (Blue Gill)	Medium to soft Low oil content	Marbled pink with darker fat line that may be removed. Lightens on cooking	Medium	Excellent smoked.
Turbot	Delicate, succulent Low to medium oil content	Apricot-coloured flesh, whitens on cooking	Delicate	
Warehou	Medium Medium to high oil content	Lightens on cooking	Full, distinct flavour	Best cooked by moist heat methods. Is ideal to incorporate in strong-flavoured dishes, e.g. curry
Whitebait	Delicate Low oil content	Whitens on cooking	Delicate—easily overpowered	
Southern Blue Whiting	Delicate, moist, easily flaked Low oil content	White	Delicate	
Albacore Tuna	Medium firm, dry High oil content	Pinkish, lightens on cooking. Whiter than Skipjack	Medium, meaty flavour	In canned form called 'Chicken of the Sea' and possesses features similar to Skipjack Tuna.
Skipjack Tuna	Medium, low moisture High oil content	Dark red flesh turns creamy brown colour when cooked	Meaty texture and flavour	Spectacular cooked whole. Excellent steaks especially when cooked in court bouillon or white wine.
Southern Bluefin Tuna	Firm, low moisture High to medium oil content	Pink to red flesh turns pinkish brown when cooked	Meaty	Ideal for sashimi.
Spiny Dogfish	Firm, boneless Medium oil content	White	Mild	Often called snow fillets in shops.

Species	Texture and Oil Content	Colour When Cooked	Flavour	Special Features
Marlin Striped/Blue and Black	Firm, low moisture High to medium oil content	Creamy pink	Meaty	Excellent smoked, often served as an entrée sashimi-style.
Rig (Spotted Dogfish)	Firm, boneless, does not flake readily Low oil content	White	Mild	Often called lemon fish in shops. Popular fish-and-chips fish.
School Shark (Grey Shark)	Firm, boneless Low oil content	White	Mild	Flesh sold as 'flake'.
Elephant Fish	Firm Low oil content	White	Medium	Sold as white fillets.
Ghost Shark	Firm Low oil content	White	Medium	Sometimes sold as pearl fillets.
Skate	Moist, delicate Medium to low oil content	White	Medium	Small skate are better than large skate. Flesh off the wings makes ideal substitute for whitebait in fritters.

SHELLFISH

Cockle	Delicate Low oil content	Cream	Delicate	Little meat in proportion to shell weight.
Pipi	Delicate Low oil content	Cream	Medium to delicate	Should be soaked in seawater for up to 24 hours to eliminate grittiness.
Toheroa	Delicate, succulent	Cream	Medium to delicate	Not usually available. Season controlled by Ministry of Agriculture and Fisheries.
Tuatua	Delicate Low oil content	Cream	Medium	Excellent as soup or chowder base.
Blue Mussel	Medium Low oil content	Cream (male), or orange (female), with black edge	Medium	Shells blue-black.
Green Mussel	Medium Low oil content	As for blue mussel	Medium	Shells varying shades of green to greenish brown.
Octopus	Firm Low oil content	White	Delicate	Ideal poached then served with seafood sauce. (Must be tenderised by beating before cooking.)
Dredge Oyster (Bluff or Nelson Oyster)	Delicate, succulent Medium oil content	Cream	Delicate when raw, medium when cooked	Flavour strengthens in proportion to time held frozen. Excellent in soup or chowder.
Pacific Oyster	Delicate, succulent Medium oil content	Cream	Delicate when raw, medium to delicate when cooked	Flesh lighter coloured than rock oyster but darker than dredge. Can be eaten raw or cooked.
Rock Oyster	Delicate Medium oil content	Cream	Sweet, delicate when raw, medium to delicate when cooked	Can be eaten raw or cooked. Keeps well, chilled in shell for up to 1 week. Smaller and sweeter than Pacific and Dredge Oysters.

Species	Texture and Oil Content	Colour When Cooked	Flavour	Special Features
Paua (Abalone)	Succulent, medium Low oil content	Black-grey exterior, white interior	Scallop-like flavour	Should be tenderised before cooking by beating. Cook whole as steaks, sliced or minced in fritters. Cook steaks only 2-3 minutes.
Scallop	As with all shellfish, scallops toughen if overcooked	Cream with orange roe	Medium to delicate	Roe provides excellent flavour for pâtés, soup or chowders.
Squid	White dense flesh, may need tenderising Low oil content	White	Delicate shellfish	Tenderise with raw kiwifruit, pawpaw or pineapple for 2-4 hours before cooking. Or blanch 1-2 minutes, then cool.
Common Swimming Crab (Paddle Crab)	Crisp, moist Low oil content	Bright white	Very sweet shellfish flavour	
Rock Lobster (Crayfish)	Crisp, meaty Low oil content	Bright white	Sweet rich flavour	

N.B. All shellfish cook very quickly and will toughen to an undesirable extent if overcooked, especially squid, paua and mussels.

STORAGE LIFE OF SEAFOOD

The storage life suggested in the following chart is a guide only and it assumes:
- that all fresh seafood is chilled at 0°C unless otherwise stated.
- that the seafood is very fresh and of a high quality at the start of its storage life.
- that the temperature for any long-term storage is -30°C.

Fresh Chilled Fish
Effective chilling is crucial for maintaining seafood at the best eating quality for the longest period of time.

The ideal temperature for fish is 0°C. To minimise the activity of enzymes and bacteria and to maximise the length of storage life and flesh quality, fresh (i.e. not frozen) fish should be chilled to 0°C.

Thermostats should be set at between 0°C and -1°C. You should not use a lower setting as this will only result in additional spoilage problems. At temperatures between -1.5°C and -5°C, fish only partially freezes. This causes a disruption of cell membranes and speeds up enzyme activity.

Shelf life and temperature
The term 'shelf life' refers to the time period that fish can be stored before it is considered unpalatable.

Fresh chilled fish has a maximum shelf life of approximately 12-14 days, beginning from the time the fish is caught. However, it must be remembered

PRODUCT	STORAGE LIFE	
	FRESH CHILLED	**FROZEN**
Fresh fish at 15°C	1 day	
5°C	3 days	
0°C	10 days	
Frozen fish at -18°C (home freezer)		3 months
-30°C (commercial)		9 months
Oysters: Dredge (Bluff), Pacific, Rock	7 days	3 months
Paua	3 days	6 months
Scallops	5 days	3 months
Squid	6 days	6 months
Mussels: Blue and Green		
Live in shell (under cover of ice)	10 days	
Cooked meat	3 days	2 months
Half shell		2 months
Shellfish: Cockle, Pipi, Toheroa, Tuatua		
Live	2 days	
Uncooked meat		3 months
Common Swimming Crab (Paddle Crab)		
Whole	2 days (live)	3 months
Meat		4 months
Rock Lobster (Crayfish)	1 day (live)	2 months
Cooked	2 days	7 months
Uncooked tails		5 months
Eel		3 months

that shelf life is entirely dependent on temperature. A shelf life of 12-14 days applies only if the fish is iced immediately it comes on board the fishing boat, and is kept at 0°C (i.e. on ice) until you buy it and cook it. Therefore, it is important to ensure that your suppliers protect and maintain the quality of their seafood.

At higher temperatures, the shelf life of fish is considerably reduced. As a rule of thumb, 1 hour at 25°C (room temperature) is equivalent to 1 day at 0°C (on ice). In other words, a fish which sits at room temperature for 4 hours has already lost 4 days' shelf life.

Also, remember that the temperature of the average refrigerator is 4°C, not 0°C. This means the shelf life of fish stored in the average refrigerator is about 6 days.

Storing large quantities of fresh chilled fish
The following steps are recommended for maximum shelf life.

1. If necessary, wash fish to remove scales or foreign matter.
2. Prepare storage container by placing a layer of ice on the base of the container. Cover with a sheet of plastic then place fillets or whole fish on the plastic. Cover with another layer of plastic then top with ice.
3. Store in chiller or refrigerator and replace ice as it melts. *N.B.* To avoid bacteria build-up in fish, and colour bleaching on the skin of whole fish, do not allow direct contact between ice and fish for any length of time.
4. If the fish has been stored on ice for 1-2 days, wash fillets before cooking.

NUMBER OF DAYS

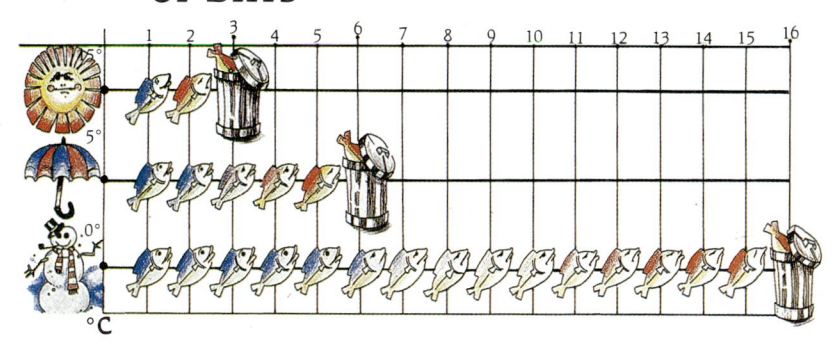

FISH

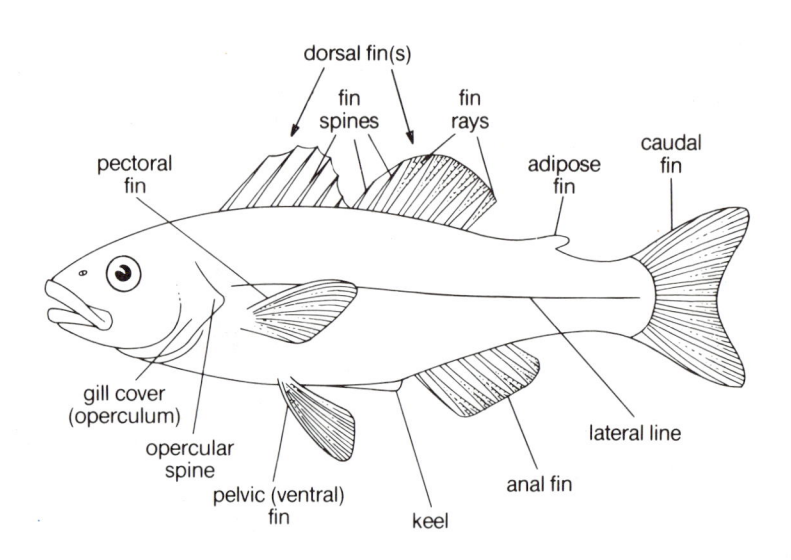

Diagram of fish anatomy with labels: dorsal fin(s), fin spines, fin rays, adipose fin, caudal fin, pectoral fin, gill cover (operculum), opercular spine, pelvic (ventral) fin, keel, anal fin, lateral line

How to Cut and Prepare Fish

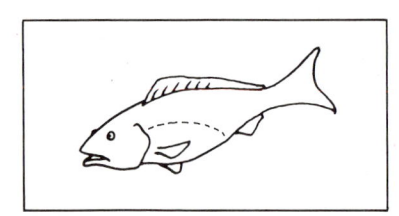

Gutted
Gutted fish are whole fish that have been gutted and sometimes scaled. Head and fins intact. A gutted fish has a longer storage life than a fish stored just as it comes from the water, because entrails cause rapid spoilage.

Dressed
Dressed fish have been scaled, gutted, and had gills removed. Head and fins are intact. A dressed fish is often cooked in one piece, by baking, poaching, or barbecuing.

Pan-dressed (Headed and Gutted)
A pan-dressed fish (more often referred to as headed and gutted) is a dressed fish with head, tail and fins removed as well.

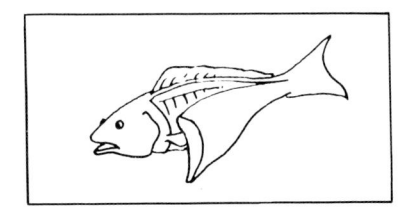

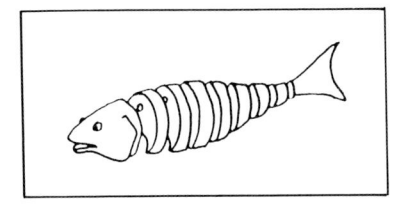

Filleted

Fillets are the boneless or 'pinbone-in' sides of a fish, cut away from the backbone and removed in one piece. In some fish, there may be pinbones radiating at right angles from the backbone. When these are removed, the fillet is boneless.

Steaked

Steaks are cross-sections cut from dressed fish. They are generally 2–4 cm thick. Large fish such as salmon, groper and mackerel are often steaked.

How to Fillet a Round-bodied Fish

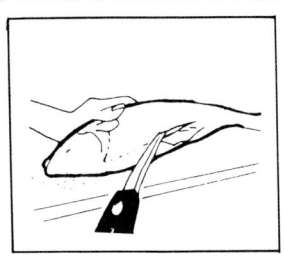

1. With fish facing away from you, use a sharp, thin-bladed knife to cut along the back of the fish, from tail to head. Make a second cut just behind the gills, down to the backbone.

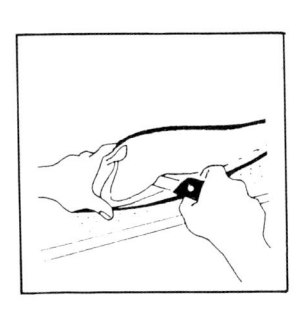

2. Holding the knife at a slight angle, cut along the bone to free the back side of the fillet.

3. Peel back the free meat, then cut fillet away from rib cage. Turn fish over and repeat this filleting process for second fillet.

How to Fillet a Flatfish

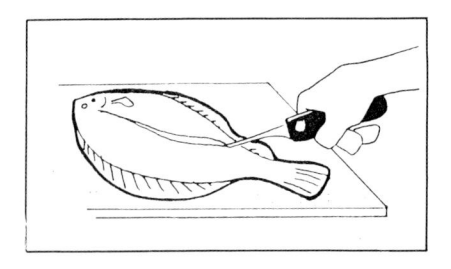

1. With the eyed (dark) side of the flatfish up, use a flexible boning knife to make a cut along the spine from the gills to the tail.

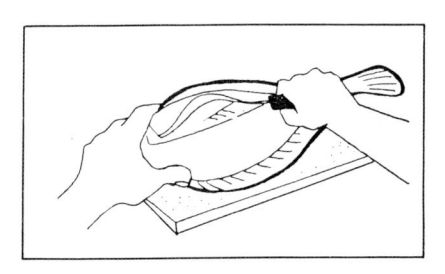

2. Slide the blade between backbone and flesh, lifting the fillet away from the bone. Remove the second fillet in the same manner.

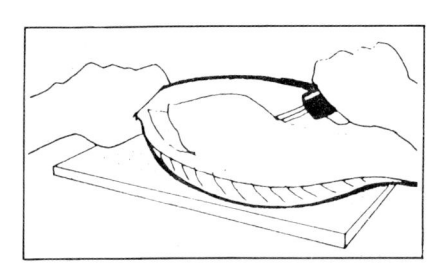

3. Turn the fish over: repeat steps 1 and 2.

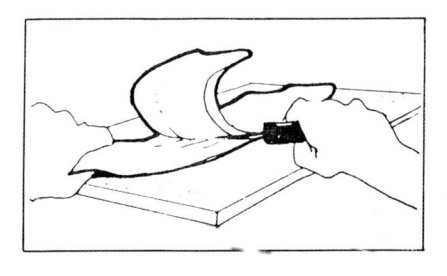

4. To skin, grasp fillet by the tail end, skin side down. Holding the knife at a slight angle, cut the meat free.

How to Steak a Round Fish

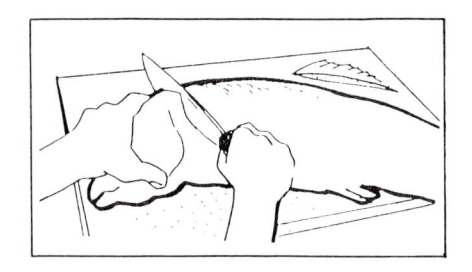

1. Remove fins from cleaned, scaled fish by running knife-point along each side of fin base, then pulling this free. To remove head, make diagonal cut behind the gills and sever backbone with heavy knife or cleaver.

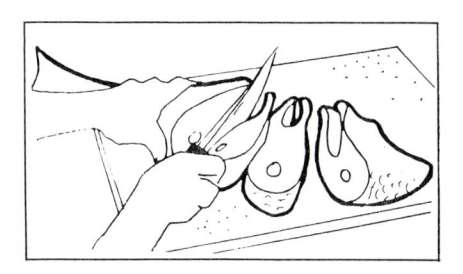

2. Still using a heavy knife, slice fish into steaks about 2-4 cm thick, starting about 11 cm from the head end. (Reserve unsteaked head and tail portions for another use.)

Methods of Cooking Fish

Fish cooks very quickly and will lose its natural succulence if overcooked. Many recipes state a certain cooking time for a given weight but this doesn't account for how the weight is distributed. A more accurate method of gauging the length of cooking time is to *measure the depth of the fish flesh at its thickest part* and use the times listed below.

Baking
This method of cooking suits all types of fish. Fillets or steaks may be baked in the oven, and baking's an excellent way to cook whole fish. The fish can be baked either 'dry' or in liquid.

Baking 'Dry'
Score the surface of the fish with a sharp knife and place in a well-oiled dish. If the fish is an oily variety, brush with lemon juice. Always baste the fish throughout cooking, until the fish is browned and tender. Bake at 180-190°C, using the times listed below as a guide.

Depth*	Fresh	Frozen
1 cm	8 minutes	17 minutes
2 cm	11 minutes	22 minutes
3 cm	15 minutes	35 minutes
4 cm	20 minutes	39 minutes

*Depth of fish flesh at thickest part

Baking in Liquid

Place fish in an ovenproof dish. Cover with liquid such as a tomato, milk or stock-based mixture. Cook at 190°C for approximately the times listed below.

Depth	Fresh	Frozen
1 cm	8 minutes	17 minutes
2 cm	11 minutes	22 minutes
3 cm	15 minutes	33 minutes
4 cm	20 minutes	36 minutes

Foil-baking or 'En Papillotte'

This method of cooking is suitable for all species.

Cut pieces of foil or greaseproof paper large enough to wrap individual fillets, steaks or whole fish. If cooking whole fish, lightly grease the foil. Season the fish with salt and pepper, fresh herbs, onion, tomato, lemon, orange or mushrooms.

Bring the edges of the foil or paper together and fold tightly to form a seal. You can also brush the paper with lightly beaten egg white to make sure the seal is airtight. Bake at 220°C using times as below.

Depth	Fresh	Frozen
1 cm	8 minutes	17 minutes
2 cm	11 minutes	22 minutes
3 cm	15 minutes	35 minutes
4 cm	20 minutes	39 minutes

Frying

Suitable for all species except some of the more oily fish.

Shallow Frying

Dry the fish then coat with seasoned flour. Do not allow the floured fish to become damp or sticky as this makes it stick to the bottom of the pan.

Fish may be floured only, or it can be battered or crumbed. It must always first be floured to make sure an extra coating sticks. If using breadcrumbs, allow the coating to set before cooking.

Depth	Fresh	Frozen
1 cm	4 minutes	7 minutes
2 cm	7 minutes	11 minutes
3 cm	10 minutes	15 minutes
4 cm	13 minutes	18 minutes

The best side of the fish should be cooked first as it will appear uppermost on the plate.

Place the fish in fat, oil or butter hot enough to seal the surface of the fish, otherwise it will absorb the cooking oil and lose its juices.

Deep Frying
Dry the fish and coat with seasoned flour then, if desired, batter, egg or egg and breadcrumbs before frying.

The fat must be hot enough to seal the surface of the fish to prevent it losing flavour and absorbing the cooking fat.

Depth	Fresh	Frozen
1 cm	3 minutes	4 minutes
2 cm	4 minutes	6 minutes
3 cm	6 minutes	10 minutes
4 cm	8 minutes	14 minutes

Grilling and Barbecuing
Suitable for most cuts and types of fish.

If using whole fish, cut gashes through the skin to allow the heat to penetrate. Brush with oil, butter or marinade to keep the fish moist during cooking. For a crisper coating, dust the fish with seasoned flour before cooking. Cook on a preheated grill or barbecue, placing the fish 5-10 cm from the source of heat.

Depth	Fresh	Frozen
1 cm	5 minutes	12 minutes
2 cm	6 minutes	15 minutes
3 cm	9 minutes	24 minutes
4 cm	11 minutes	28 minutes

Steaming
Suitable for all types of fish. Place the seasoned fish in a perforated steamer or on a heatproof plate over a saucepan of gently boiling water. The fish must be covered tightly during cooking.

Depth	Fresh	Frozen
1 cm	3 minutes	5 minutes
2 cm	7 minutes	11 minutes
3 cm	11 minutes	13 minutes
4 cm	14 minutes	16 minutes

Poaching

Suitable for all species, although take care with delicate-textured species. Poached fish is cooked in a seasoned liquid held at just below boiling point (i.e. simmering). The simmering temperature for water is usually 93-95°C; the boiling point is 100°C.

Whole fish should be poached by placing the fish in cold liquid, bringing it to just below boiling point and simmering until cooked. If the fish is to be served cold, bring the fish to boiling point then remove the pan from the heat and allow the fish to cool in the poaching liquid.

Cuts of fish should be placed in a simmering liquid. This effectively 'seals' the fish and stops the juices from escaping and coagulating into a white coating on the cut surface of the fish.

Fish may be shallow or deep poached. When fish is shallow poached, the cooking liquid barely covers the fish and it is usually used to make a sauce.

Times given below are for *cuts of fish* placed in hot poaching liquid.

Depth	Fresh	Frozen
1 cm	8 minutes	10 minutes
2 cm	10 minutes	15 minutes
3 cm	12 minutes	22 minutes
4 cm	13 minutes	28 minutes

Microwaving

Suitable for all types of fish.

Arrange fish in a shallow serving dish with the thickest parts to the outside edges of the dish. If you wish, brush the fish with butter or lemon juice or cover it with sauce. Don't add salt or pepper before cooking — this often overpowers the natural seafood flavour.

Cover the dish with a damp paper towel or plastic wrapping with holes for ventilation to keep the fish moist while cooking. If cooking from frozen use the low or defrost power range to start, then cook at normal power. Fish that contains a high percentage of water should be cooked at a lower power and pierced several times with a fork to allow the steam to escape. It's advisable to test the fish by gently cooking it. Lower the power and pierce the fish if it starts to explode or spit while cooking.

Don't use the microwave to shallow or deep fry or to reheat fried foods as the coating doesn't turn crisp and using fat in a microwave is too dangerous.

Calculating cooking time for a microwave is more complicated than for conventional cooking methods. This is because cooking time in a microwave depends on both the thickness of the fish and the overall quantity of fish being cooked. For instance, 500 g fish 2 cm thick will take longer to cook than 200 g fish of the same thickness.

As well, the temperature of food cooked in a microwave actually rises when the food is taken out of the microwave, and it continues to cook on standing.

For this reason, and because a microwave cooks extremely quickly anyway, it is better to underestimate the cooking time for fish, rather than overestimating and running the risk of overcooking the fish.

Cooking times for 1 fillet (150 g) of fish:

Depth	Fresh	Frozen
1 cm	1 minute	1 minute defrost 1½ minutes cook
2 cm	1½ minutes	1 minute defrost 2 minutes cook
3 cm	2½ minutes	2 minutes defrost 2½ minutes cook
4 cm	3 minutes	2 minutes defrost 3 minutes cook

Sousing

Suitable for all medium- to firm-textured species. It is an ideal method of cooking fish to be served cold with salads. Soused fish may be stored for up to a week in the refrigerator.

Make a sousing liquid of vinegar or wine, herbs or spices, bring it to the boil and simmer 10 minutes. Place the fish in a non-aluminium pan and add the liquid. Cook either in the oven or on top of the stove. Cool the fish in the liquid, store covered in the refrigerator for at least 1 day before using, to allow flavours to penetrate. Drain before serving.

Marinating

Suitable for medium- to firm-textured fish.

The principle of marinating is that the acidic marinade used alters the structure of the seafood protein and its colour as heat would, and therefore no cooking is required.

Marinating works best with skinned and boned fish, or fillets.

Cut the fish into cubes of about 1.5 cm, or larger if you wish. Place the cubes in a non-aluminium bowl or strong plastic bag with fresh herbs or thick slices of onion. Add the juice of oranges, lemons or other citrus fruit — or wine or vinegar. Cover and place in the refrigerator. Marinate 4-6 hours for 1.5 cm cubes and 6-8 hours or overnight for larger cubes.

Drain marinade and serve the fish with seafood sauce or coconut cream. The marinade may be re-used immediately as long as it's been under refrigeration, but it should not be held for a total of more than 2 days in the refrigerator.

Frozen fish need not be thawed before placing in marinade. Leave the frozen fish at room temperature only long enough to make it easy to cut. Add 1-2 hours on to the marinating time to allow the fish to thaw.

FROZEN FISH

Buying Frozen Fish

Frozen fish is extremely useful and convenient. The type of fish you want may not always be available chilled, but you can buy frozen fish in advance and keep it frozen until you need it. If the fish has been correctly packaged and stored, the cooked dish should be almost indistinguishable from one made from good quality chilled fish. In many cases, frozen fish is of better quality than chilled fish which may have been incorrectly handled and stored.

As well as smaller consumer packs of frozen fish, bulk packs are generally available in 10 kg cartons. The fish should either be layer-packed with plastic sheets in between or the fillets should be individually wrapped in plastic. Don't buy fish frozen in block form as it will be difficult to separate the individual fillets.

What to Look For

Before you buy or use frozen fish, open the cartons and check the following points:

- The pack itself should be intact with no damage to the seals or the outer wrapping.
- Fillets should be solidly frozen with no discolouration or brownish tonings.
- The fish should not smell — a strong fishy odour may indicate poor quality and poor freezing.
- There should be no sign of defrosting and refreezing, so avoid packs containing large amounts of ice within the package, or badly distorted fish or fillets.
- The colour of the fat varies from species to species, but in general it should be dark brown. It lightens on storage to a light brown, creamy colour.
- White or bleached patches on the flesh are a sign of freezer burn or dehydrated flesh.

Storing Frozen Fish

Frozen fish should be kept frozen solid until it is needed. Do not refreeze fish that has been thawed. Refrigerate it and use as soon as possible.

Commercial freezers can hold fish at below -30°C. This is ideal for long-term storage because the denaturation of proteins, oxidation of fats and enzyme or bacterial action are all reduced greatly at this temperature.

Domestic freezers hold fish at approximately -18°C which is suitable for short-term storage only. It is not cold enough to maintain the quality of the fish. Fish should be stored for no longer than 2 months, and preferably only 1 month, at this temperature.

It is better to buy commercially frozen fish than to freeze it yourself. If you have to freeze fish, it must be of good quality, frozen rapidly and used as soon as possible (within 1 month).

Take Care of Your Frozen Fish
To retain top quality, fish must be correctly stored and frozen.

Texture
Protein can be denatured by enzyme action. This means that the proteins lose their natural structure and thus their ability to 'hold' water. Once thawed, the flesh drips excessively and looks dull white and spongy. When cooked, the fish tastes wet and sloppy. Denaturation occurs if the freezing process is slow or if the temperature fluctuates to any extent during freezing and storage.

Another detrimental effect of slow freezing is that the water in the cells separates out and accumulates, forming large ice crystals which puncture cell walls. This results in changes in the texture of the flesh.

From -1.5°C to -3°C is the critical stage for freezing fish as enzyme action increases markedly. This temperature range must be passed through as quickly as possible.

Fats
Fish fats will become rancid if the storage temperatures are too high, if the fish has insufficient protective packaging, or no ice glaze to prevent air from reaching the fish flesh. Rancidity affects the flavours and odours of fish. These 'off' flavours vary from mild cod liver oil to a burnt or paint taste.

Freezer burn
'Freezer burn' or dehydration occurs during frozen storage if the temperature fluctuates and there is air inside the wrapping.

On occasions the wrapper may be cooler than the fish and the moisture may leave the fish and condense on the inside of the wrapper. This moisture forms ice crystals in the package and the surface of the fish becomes white and dehydrated. The flesh when cooked is spongy and dry.

Cooking Frozen Fish
For the best results, frozen fish should be cooked while still frozen or icy (before it starts to drip). This poses no real problems as fish can be cooked by all methods from a frozen state by adapting the recipe slightly and cooking for longer at a slightly lower temperature. As a general rule of thumb, add an extra 10 minutes to the cooking times given under 'Methods of Cooking Fish' on page 25 for each 2.5 cm of thickness of fillet.

Thawing Frozen Fish
If you're forced to thaw fish, the most satisfactory method is to place fish or fillets in a container and put them in the bottom of the refrigerator for several hours or overnight. *Do not* leave fish on a bench top to defrost as its quality will rapidly deteriorate and the fish will develop 'off' flavours very quickly.

WHOLE FISH

With a whole fish you can easily prepare wonderful dishes that look as though you have gone to a lot of trouble, when in reality the preparation and cooking have been extremely simple.

Most fish can be cooked whole. The fish most commonly cooked in this way include northern kingfish (yellowtail), tarakihi, snapper, kahawai, creamfish (leatherjacket), blue moki, mackerel, warehou, mullet, flounder, sole, trevally, butterfish, gurnard, tuna, blue cod, salmon and tuna (small).

When preparing whole fish for cooking, first scale the fish, if necessary. This is most easily done using a spoon held so that the scales collect in it as it is scraped against the scales. Scale the fish in a tub of water (this stops the scales ending up on the ceiling and down the back of the fridge!).

Remove the gut, wash the gut cavity and then remove the head if you wish. You can also remove the gills as this prevents the gill flavour from permeating the rest of the fish.

Now that your fish is ready to be cooked, a host of options await. You can souse the fish and serve it cold, steam and serve it Chinese style, foil-bake it (perhaps the easiest way of cooking whole fish), or stuff and bake it for a succulent savoury dish. For cooking times see 'Methods of Cooking Fish' page 25. If you have a frozen whole fish in the freezer, defrost it in the refrigerator until it reaches the pliable icy stage — don't allow it to start dripping. Add a few minutes to the cooking time, depending on the size of the fish.

When it comes to serving and eating the whole fish, look at it and work out where the bones are and take the meat from them. Many people inexperienced in serving whole fish just panic and dive in, creating great turmoil and bones with each mouthful!

Times for Grilling and Barbecuing
Cut gashes through the skin of the whole fish to allow heat to penetrate.

Depth	Cooking Time
1 cm	5 minutes
2 cm	6 minutes
3 cm	9 minutes
4 cm	11 minutes

SMOKED SEAFOOD

Many people enjoy the flavour that smoking gives to seafood. Most species of fish and shellfish may be smoked and this process transforms the seafood into a delicious, succulent product that is very tempting. If the fish is hot-smoked it may be eaten without further cooking — ideal for picnics and lunches with fresh sliced bread rolls or perhaps accompanied by a salad for dinner.

To make thin slicing of smoked fish easier, partially freeze the fillet or fish prior to cutting with a very sharp knife.

Cold-smoked Fish
This is smoked at a low temperature and the flesh remains uncooked in the smoking process. The exterior of cold-smoked fish is golden orange and the flesh translucent. Uncooked cold-smoked fish can be served thinly sliced if it is very fresh, or cooked in any dish requiring smoked fish. Cold-smoked fish may be stored, covered, in the refrigerator for up to 2 days. Home freezing is recommended for up to 1 month only. For methods of cooking smoked fish, refer to 'Methods of Cooking Fish' page 25. All cooking methods except sousing and marinating are suitable.

Hot-smoked Fish
Hot-smoked fish is smoked at a much higher temperature than cold-smoked fish and the flesh is cooked during the smoking process, so it may be eaten without further cooking. Hot-smoked fish has a golden brown appearance, and the flesh is opaque and may be a little drier than cold-smoked fish. It may be added to hot dishes but only requires heating through. Hot-smoked fish may be stored, covered, in the refrigerator for up to 3 days or may be frozen for up to 3 months.

Remember that the characteristic texture of the seafood is not markedly altered by the smoking process, so choose the species most suited to your recipe. For example, if you wish to flake the smoked fish for fish cakes or a pie, choose a delicate- or medium-textured fish. If you want to make a chowder with cubes of smoked fish in it, choose a firm-textured fish, such as lemon fish or ling.

SHELLFISH

Many of us have spent warm summer evenings gathering shellfish at the beach. Memories of these times with friends or family often dominate our thoughts as we spend long winter evenings by the fire.

But why enjoy such treats only when you visit the beach? Obtain shellfish from your seafood retailer and make a chowder or paella, or deep fry them for a quick but delicious meal.

Shellfish such as surf clams, tuatuas, pipis and blue and green mussels are cooked by steaming, poaching, barbecuing, baking or microwaving to open them. They can either be eaten as is or added to other dishes and heated through.

Oysters, paua, scallops and sea eggs (kina) are shucked (opened) when raw and the meat extracted.

If you do collect your own shellfish from around the coast, ensure that the area is free from pollution. If in doubt, check with the fisheries officer at the Ministry of Agriculture and Fisheries office nearest you.

To flush sand and grit from freshly gathered shellfish, leave them in a bucket of clear salt water in a cool place for at least 24 hours.

Storing Shellfish

Shellfish die if they are stored at temperatures that are either too high or too low. If they are covered with fresh water for a long period of time they will drown. To test if mussels, cockles or pipis are alive before cooking, leave them at room temperature for 20 minutes then tap lightly or hold under fresh running water until they close. If the shell remains open about 1 cm, the shellfish is dead — discard it.

Mussels, Cockles, Pipis

For the best quality and shelf life, live mussels and other bivalves should be stored between 2°C and 4°C under a cover of melting ice. It is important that the ice does not make direct contact with the shellfish.

Place the shellfish in a container (preferably one with drainage holes), cover with a towel or sacking, and then cover with ice. The container should be kept in a cool spot but not in the refrigerator. The melting ice keeps the shellfish at the correct temperature but the water must be drained off and the ice replenished. The shellfish may be kept for a short time in the warmer part of the refrigerator, but their quality is not maintained when they're stored like this.

Scallops and Oysters

Scallops and oysters are generally purchased out of the shell. They should be stored in the refrigerator and used as soon as possible.

Frozen Shellfish

Shellfish, like fish, are best if frozen commercially but even then they cannot be kept in the freezer indefinitely. If you freeze them domestically, use only top quality shellfish, freeze as quickly as possible and protect with freezer-proof packaging.

Before you use or buy frozen shellfish, check the following points:

- The pack itself should be intact with no damage to the seals or the outer wrapping.
- General appearance — shellfish should be solidly frozen and not damaged or broken.
- The shellfish should not smell — a strong odour can indicate poor quality and poor freezing.
- There should be no sign of defrosting and refreezing, so avoid packs containing large amounts of ice within the package.
- Bleached, lighter and dehydrated patches on the flesh are a sign of freezer burn.

How to Clean and Prepare Shellfish
How to Shuck an Oyster

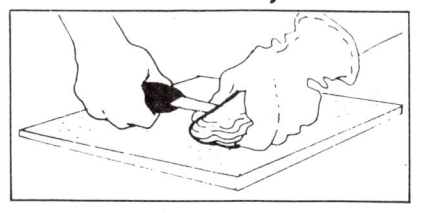

1. Hold oysters under cold running water and scrub with a stiff brush; discard those that are not tightly closed or that do not close quickly when handled. Place oyster, cupped side down, on a firm surface, holding it (with a gloved hand) near the hinge.

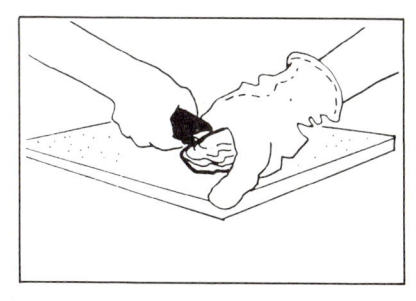

2. Insert an oyster knife in the side opposite the hinge, and twist knife blade to force oyster open.

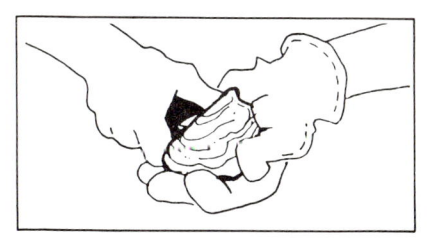

3. Run the knife around the edge of the shell to cut the muscle that holds the two shells together.

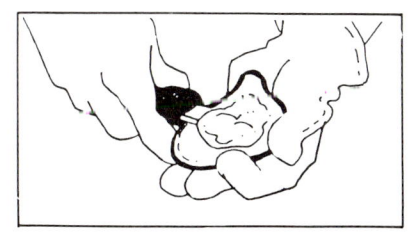

4. Remove top shell, and loosen oyster from bottom shell. Check for shell fragments before serving.

How to Clean a Mussel

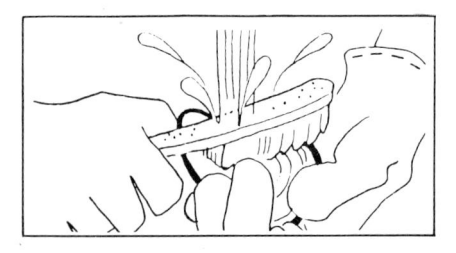

1. Hold mussels under cold running water and scrub with a stiff brush.

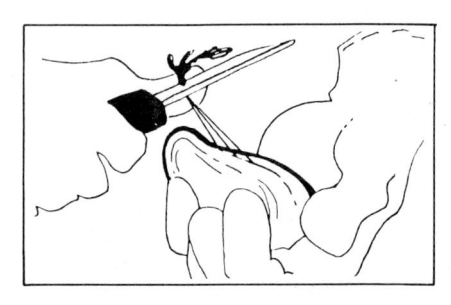

2. Clip or pull beard. Rinse mussel before cooking.

How to Open Scallops, Cockles, Pipis, Tuatuas and Other Surf Clams

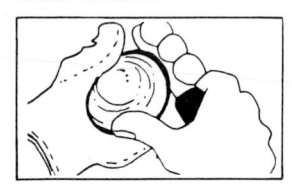

1. Wash thoroughly, discarding any that have broken shells or that do not close. Wearing a heavy glove for safety, hold the shellfish in your palm and force the blade of a short knife between the shells. Hold the scallop cupped-side down.

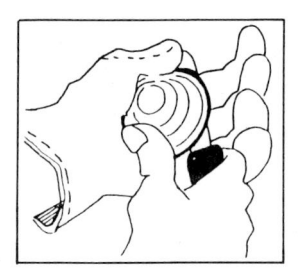

2. Run the knife around the edge of the shell to cut through the muscles holding it together.

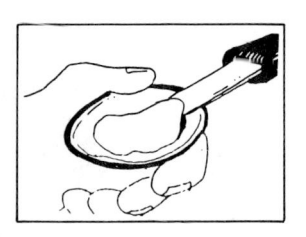

3. Open shellfish and remove top shell. Use knife to loosen meat from bottom shell. Keep only the roe and white meat of scallops; throw the rest away. Check all shellfish for shell fragments before using.

N.B. Cockles, tuatuas, pipis, and other surf clams, like mussels, are best opened by steaming.

Cooking Shellfish

Baking
Baking in liquid or a sauce is preferable to dry-baking as it prevents the shellfish from drying out, overcooking and becoming tough.

Oysters and scallops, which are normally bought raw, will take longer to cook than previously cooked meats such as mussels, which only need to be heated through before serving.

Cooking times will be affected by the temperature of the sauce or liquid to which the shellfish are added. Obviously, shellfish added to a hot liquid will require a shorter cooking time.

Frying
Suitable for all types of shellfish.

Shallow Frying
Coat the shellfish in seasoned flour before cooking. Shellfish may be cooked in either oil or butter or a mixture of both, and flavoured with garlic, herbs or other ingredients. The shellfish should be placed in hot oil (180°C) or butter to seal the outside and prevent the shellfish from absorbing excess oil and losing its juices and flavour. The length of cooking time again depends on whether the shellfish is raw or has been steamed open, but the aim is to cook the shellfish as rapidly as possible. Long cooking results in a tough, dry product.

Deep Frying
Dry the shellfish and coat with seasoned flour then, if desired, batter, egg or egg and breadcrumbs before frying.

It is preferable to dust seafood with flour to dry it out before coating it with batter or egg. This helps the coating to stick well.

Uncooked shellfish, such as scallops
- Fresh   2-3 minutes
- Frozen   4 minutes

Cooked shellfish, such as mussels
- Fresh   1-2 minutes
- Frozen   3 minutes

Marinating
Pre-cooked shellfish, such as mussels that have been steamed open, may be placed in an acid-based marinade (vinegar, lemon juice, wine) and kept chilled overnight before serving. The more acid in the marinade, the sooner the shellfish will be ready to eat. The acid helps preserve them and domestically marinated shellfish, especially mussels, may be stored chilled up to 7 days before eating. For health reasons, all shellfish should be lightly cooked before marinating.

Grilling and Barbecuing

More suitable for raw shellfish such as oysters, scallops and prawns than for pre-cooked shellfish meats. Brush or dot with oil or butter to keep the shellfish moist during cooking. Place over a preheated barbecue, or under a grill or salamander — they must be hot enough to seal the shellfish instantly. Place the shellfish 5-10 cm from the source of the heat. Shellfish may be marinated before being cooked to enhance flavour and increase moistness.

Uncooked shellfish, such as scallops
- Fresh   2-3 minutes
- Frozen   4-5 minutes

Cooked shellfish, such as mussels (use a slightly higher heat)
- Fresh   1-2 minutes
- Frozen   3-4 minutes

Poaching

All shellfish, whether fresh, frozen or still in the shell, can be poached. The poaching liquid can be a stock, seasoned water or wine mixture. Bring the liquid to simmering point then add the shellfish. Keep the liquid simmering.

Shellfish still in the shell are cooked as soon as the shells open 1-2 cm. Other shellfish such as scallops, prawns and oysters require only a short cooking time (2-3 minutes) at simmering point.

Steaming

Steaming shellfish open produces a moist result and with the use of wine and herbs in the cooking liquid a delicious flavour is imparted.

To steam in a saucepan, place about 1 cm water or dry white wine and water in a large saucepan.

Add flavourings such as parsley stalks, onions, ground black pepper etc.

Place the scrubbed shellfish into the liquid, cover with a tight-fitting lid and bring to the boil.

Reduce to simmering and cook until the shellfish open 1-2 cm. This takes approximately 2-3 minutes if the shellfish are small and longer for large shellfish. Do not overcook or the shellfish will toughen.

Retain the liquid and use as a base for a sauce, soup, chowder or casserole.

Shellfish may also be steamed open by placing in a steamer over gently boiling water.

Microwaving

Suitable for all types of shellfish as it retains the flavour. The suggested cooking times given below are for quantities of about 6 shellfish.

Live mussels and similar shellfish should be placed in the microwave and cooked on medium-high power for 2-3 minutes. The mussels are ready as soon as the shells open 1-2 cm.

Scallop meats should be pierced several times with a fork to allow steam to escape during cooking. Cover with a damp paper towel and cook on medium power for 2-3 minutes.

Oyster meats must be pierced several times with a skewer or fork to allow steam to escape during cooking. Oysters are best cooked with a topping to prevent them drying out. Cook on medium power for about 1½-2 minutes. Don't overcook or the oysters will toughen.

CRABS

Crabs should be purchased live or freshly cooked. If buying them live, make sure their legs and claws are moving vigorously. When buying cooked crabs check that the legs or claws spring back when unfolded and released. If they hang limp they've been handled incorrectly.

Crabs shed their shells many times before reaching maturity. If the crab has a pale shell and feels light or hollow, it may have recently shed its shell and the meat will not be in good condition. An average-sized crab, about 10 cm across the back of its shell, will yield 85 to 100 g crab meat.

Once purchased or gathered from the beach, crabs should be stored alive at between 1°C and 7°C, prior to preparation and cooking. The cooked meat can be packed into plastic freezer containers, and frozen for up to 1 month.

Fresh chilled or frozen meat may be purchased but it has to be cooked before being eaten. The fresh chilled crab meat should be used as soon as possible but the frozen meat can be stored in the deep freeze for up to 4 months.

Cooking Crab

New Zealand paddle crabs are smaller than many species of crab and the meat that they contain is more easily removed if they are first cooked.

Firstly drown the crabs in fresh cool water and then prepare by one of the following methods.

Poaching

Bring a large saucepan of water to the boil, adding 1 tsp salt for every litre of water.

Add a few sprigs of parsley and a strip of lemon to the water.

Drop crabs into the boiling water and simmer whole crabs for 8-10 minutes, or cleaned sections for 4-5 minutes. (These times are approximate and vary according to the size of the crabs. For smaller crabs reduced times should be used.)

Once cooked, chill immediately by immersing in cold water for 2-3 minutes to prevent flesh from overcooking.

Refrigerate until ready to use. If storing whole, break off the tail section and store on end to allow juices to drain.

Steaming

Steaming ensures a good retention of natural flavours.

Place the crabs over boiling water, allowing 10-12 minutes for whole crabs and 6-8 minutes for sectioned crabs.

Cool immediately in cold running water. Refrigerate.

Microwaving

Place whole or sectioned crabs in a microwave-proof dish.

Cook on high power for 3-4 minutes.

Chill immediately under cold running water.

How to Remove Crab Meat

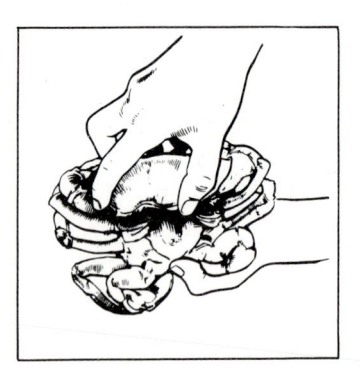

1. Lift the top shell off the cooked crab with a quick movement starting at the tail.

2. Remove and discard the grey stomach, mouth parts and spongy pointed gills.

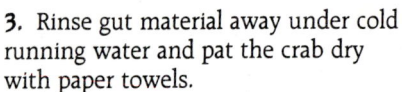

3. Rinse gut material away under cold running water and pat the crab dry with paper towels.

4. Remove the tail flap. (The tail sections are a maze of crevices.)

5. Remove the claws. Crack them open and remove the meat.

6. Break the remaining crab in half.

7. Holding one half section of the crab by the legs, place it body side down on the chopping board and using a rolling pin start from the legs and work towards the body rolling the meat. Repeat with the other half of the crab.

8. Nothing remains but the meat and shell. Remove any small pieces of shell from the recovered meat.

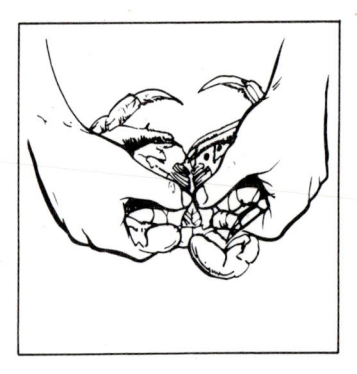

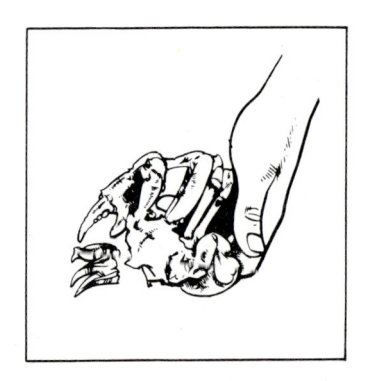

PRAWNS AND SHRIMPS

How to Dress a Raw Prawn (or Shrimp)

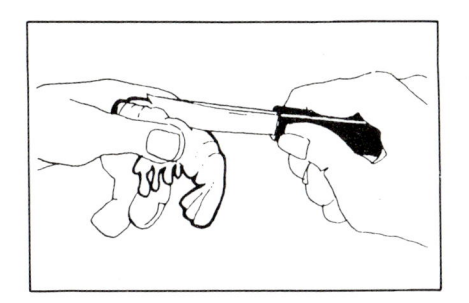

1. With a sharp knife, make a shallow cut along the back of the prawn, from head to tail. Peel off shell and legs, leaving the shell on the tail, if desired. To remove vein, hold prawn under cold running water. The water will help rinse out the vein.

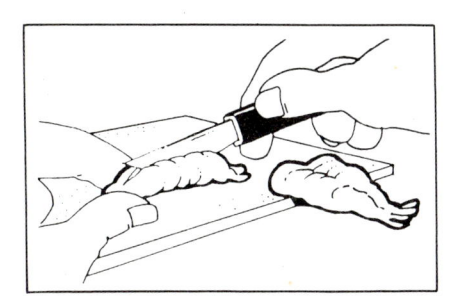

2. To butterfly, cut along the back of the prawn, but not all the way through. Spread the halves open.

Cooking Prawns and Shrimps

Most prawns and shrimps are purchased cooked, i.e. they are a soft pink colour as opposed to the shiny brown colour of the fresh product.

If purchased raw they may be cooked by microwaving on medium to high power (prawns take 4-5 minutes usually) or by simmering gently in a saucepan of water.

ROCK LOBSTER (Crayfish)

Rock lobsters, commonly called crayfish, should be purchased live or freshly cooked. When buying them live, choose energetic ones which flap vigorously when picked up — don't choose lethargic ones. When buying cooked lobsters look at the tail — it should be tucked firmly up against the underside of the body and if you straighten it out the tail should snap back into place when it is released. If the tail is hanging limp, it's a fair indication the lobster has been handled incorrectly or has died too long before cooking.

If rock lobsters are purchased live they are best killed as soon as possible because enzymic action causes great change in the flavour and texture of the flesh.

Rock lobsters may be killed by:

- *Drowning.* Place in fresh cold water for about 20 minutes. Once dead, cook the lobster as soon as possible.
- *Chilling.* Place in a freezer for about 30 minutes. This slows down the lobster, making it easy to handle, and it can then be cooked (in boiling water or stock) or killed by knifing.
- *Knifing.* Hold lobster underside down on a bench or board and quickly pierce between the eyes with a sharp knife or cleaver. Continue the cut down through the full length of the body and tail. Alternatively, remove the tail by cutting through the soft part where the tail joins the body.

Do not kill lobsters by plunging the live creature into boiling water — it causes the legs to drop off and the flesh to toughen.

How to Prepare Rock Lobster for Grilling

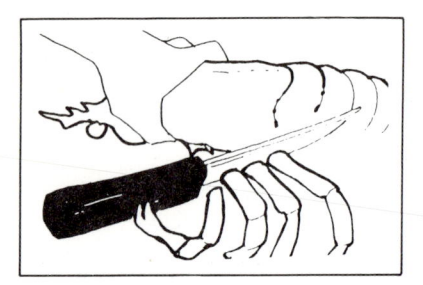

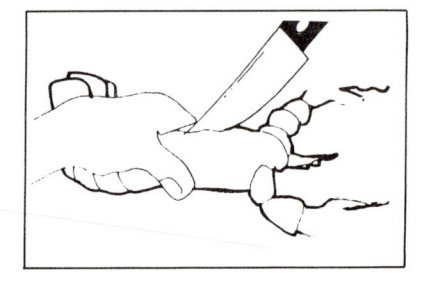

1. Kill first by drowning or knifing. Cut off legs.
2. Insert a knife in the abdomen, and cut through the undershell toward the head, leaving back shell intact.

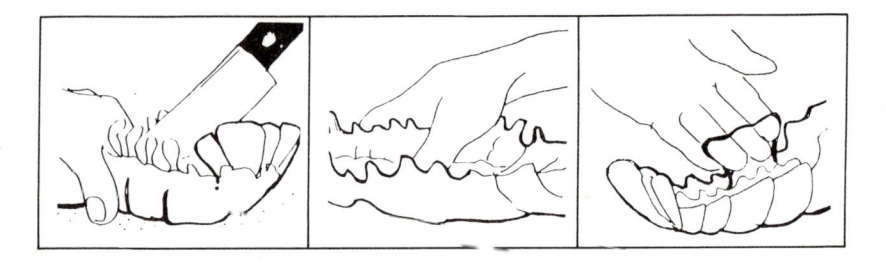

3. Cut toward the tail.
4. Press the lobster apart.
5. Remove sand sac from head; remove intestinal tract.

Cooking Rock Lobster

Microwaving
Microwave on a medium to high power and turn once during cooking. Halfway through, cover or shield the legs (according to manufacturer's suggestions) to prevent overcooking. The length of time will vary depending on the weight of the lobster.

After cooking allow at least 2 minutes rest/recovery before serving or preparing further.

If using frozen rock lobster, defrost in the refrigerator for 12 hours or in the microwave on a low setting, turning once, for 6 minutes.

To cook, microwave on high setting for 7 minutes, turning once during cooking. Allow 2 minutes rest/recovery before serving or preparing further.

For best results microwave 1 at a time.

Boiling
Bring a saucepan of water (large enough to allow movement of the rock lobster body) to the boil. Place the rock lobster into the saucepan and simmer until it turns bright red and the flesh has turned from translucent to pearly white.

Chopped onion, carrot and celery may be added to the water for flavouring. Reserve the stock for sauces or casseroles or freeze for later use.

When cooked, plunge the rock lobster into ice-cold water to prevent further cooking and then drain. The meat may be eaten cold or added to other cold or hot dishes.

If using frozen rock lobster, thaw first in refrigerator for 12 hours and then boil as for fresh lobster.

Grilling
Prepare the rock lobster as shown on page 42. The following instructions are for a tail weighing 200 g — for a heavier tail, increase the cooking time by a few minutes.

To cook: place the tail, shell side up, on a baking tray or grill pan. Preheat the grill to 200°C and placing the rock lobster tail 15-20 cm from the grill, cook for 4-5 minutes. Turn over and cook a further 4-5 minutes until the flesh turns opaque throughout.

SQUID

How to Prepare Squid

Of the two species of squid common to New Zealand waters the main commercial species is the arrow squid (pictured). The broad mantle squid, which has a slightly different appearance, is less common. Squid normally have a year-long life cycle. Young, small squid are tender and delicious, when cooked according to directions. However, larger squid (with tube length more than 14 cm) may require tenderising before cooking, by blanching or marinating.

Squid are available either fresh or frozen; whole, or cleaned and ready to cook. The three main parts of a squid are 1) the tail or fin; 2) tube, hood or mantle; and 3) the head, gut and tentacles.

There are two preparation methods:

Method A

1. Hold the tube in one hand. With the other hand gently pull back the transparent 'backbone' so the tube and gut become separated. Pull out gut (still attached to head). Remove the 'backbone' from inside the tube.

2. Lay tentacles with head and gut attached on chopping board. Cut off tentacles where they join the head. (Discard head and gut or use for bait.) Cut suckers off with knife or scissors or rub off if squid is young. Lay tube with tail facing downwards on chopping board. Cut tail off.

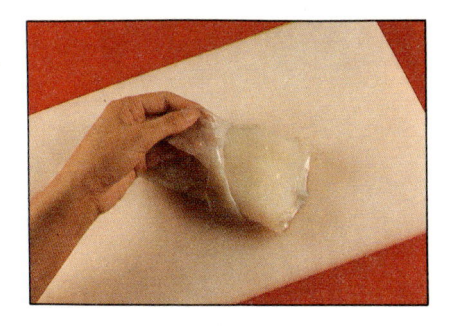

3. If white rather than pink cooked flesh is required, peel the skin off (salt hands for good grip). Alternatively, rub skin off with pumice stone.

4. Cut off the narrow ring of cartilage around the top of the tube. Rinse the tube under cold running water. Slice into rings, strips, cubes or leave whole.

Method B

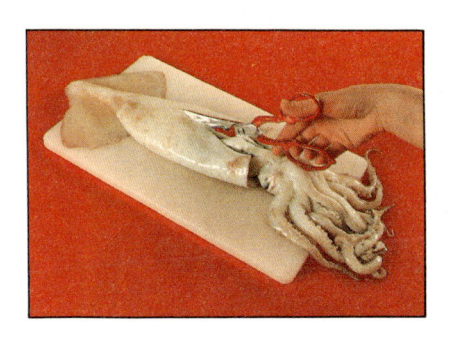

Cut open the tube from the opening to the tail with kitchen scissors. Open tube out. Remove gut and backbone. Proceed as from (2) in Method A.

The washed tentacles and tail may be prepared by chopping and frying in hot oil (180°C) for 20-30 seconds only. Alternatively they may be minced and used in fritters or patties, or added to a fish soup.

Tenderising Squid

If the squid tube is large (over 14 cm), it may require tenderising by marinating or blanching before cooking.

Marinating

After cleaning the squid, place in a plastic bag with ½ raw peeled kiwifruit or a slice of raw crushed pineapple or pawpaw for at least 1 hour. (These 3 fruits contain an enzyme which tenderises protein. The fruit must be raw and ripe when used. The colour and flavour of the squid remains unaffected by the action of the fruit.)

Blanching

Alternatively, blanching the cleaned squid greatly increases the tenderness of the flesh. Simply immerse cleaned squid tube which has been cut as desired or left whole, into a bowl of hot, but not boiling, water. Stir once or twice.

After 2 minutes immediately remove from water and cool under cold running water for a few seconds.

Refrigerate until ready to cook.

Cooking times given in recipes must still be followed closely to prevent overcooking and subsequent toughening even if tenderised squid is used.

SASHIMI

There is increasing interest in Japanese methods of preparing and serving seafoods and we can learn much from this artistic approach to food.

Sashimi is a traditional Japanese dish and consists of small, very thinly sliced pieces of raw fish.

Fish such as New Zealand's top quality snapper and albacore and bluefin tuna fetch high prices on the Japanese market where they are sold for sashimi.

Fish with darker flesh such as tuna are the most commonly used, but white-fleshed fish and seafoods such as shrimp, squid and abalone are also served sashimi-style.

Sashimi is traditionally served with soy sauce and wasabi (Japanese horseradish). When served in restaurants it is usually eaten as one of several courses, whereas at home it would be served with sake or a side dish of rice.

True sashimi is sliced very thinly and it is said that the ability to slice the fish into sashimi is a true test of the fish retailer's or chef's skill. It may take many years to acquire this skill and to assist them, those preparing sashimi use a long, thin, single-edged knife especially designed for the task.

Sashimi is usually served on a flat plate or maybe in a shallow bowl containing a layer of thinly shredded Japanese radish.

Garnishes include the aromatic green shio leaves (beefsteak plant) or edible chrysanthemum flowers, together with the wasabi. Freshly grated ginger or lemon slices are also used.

The art of eating sashimi is as important as its preparation. The sashimi is dipped into soy sauce in which wasabi has been dissolved or else a small amount of wasabi is dabbed on to the fish before placing it in the soy sauce.

MICROWAVE MAGIC

Seafood dishes cooked in a microwave oven are succulent and delicious. The natural colour and flavour of fish and shellfish are enhanced by microwaving and once you have tried cooking seafood in your microwave oven you're sure to be converted.

Basic Hints
- Use only those utensils and implements recommended for use with your microwave oven.
- *Do not attempt* to deep or shallow fry any food in a microwave oven as the fat or oil temperature cannot be controlled.
- If the quantity of food cooked in a microwave oven is increased, the cooking time must also increase.

Preparation
- For best results, prepare seafood at the last minute before serving.
- As the flavour of food is more intense when cooked in a microwave oven, add only small quantities of seasonings to food before cooking.

Cooking
- Cook fish covered, unless coated with breadcrumbs which seal in the juices. Suitable coverings include paper towels, waxed paper, or plastic wrap which must have one edge turned back or be pierced to let excess steam escape.
- The cooking time for fish increases with the firmness of the flesh, thus soft-fleshed fish, such as hoki, red cod or flounder, will cook more quickly than firm-fleshed fish, such as groper, ling or lemon fish.
- Overcooking dries and toughens seafoods, so cook for the minimum time recommended in the recipe, then check to see if it is ready.
- As food continues to cook when taken from the microwave oven, *always* allow a *standing time* which allows the seafood to finish cooking. Standing time should be approximately one-third of the cooking time.
- When fish is done, the flesh turns opaque and should barely flake with a fork (the centre may still be slightly translucent).
- When preparing seafood recipes ahead of time, undercook slightly and then finish off cooking in the microwave on high just before serving.
- *Whole fish* can be cooked:
  1. without any additional liquid, or
  2. with a little melted butter or lemon juice, or
  3. stuffed.
- *Fish fillets or steaks* may be:
  1. Steamed without any additional liquid or with a little melted butter or lemon juice.
  2. Poached in a liquid such as lemon juice, wine, stock, milk, water or sauce.

3. Grilled in a browning dish after coating the fish with seasoned flour, a batter, or crumbs.
- *Shellfish* are delicious cooked and served in their own natural containers. To microwave mussels, oysters, scallops, tuatuas, pipis in their shells:
  1. Scrub and rinse shells under cold running water to remove sand.
  2. Place 8-10 in a circle on microwave tray. Cover.
  3. Microwave on high 2-4 minutes until shells open 1-2 cm. Any shells unopened after this time probably contain dead shellfish and should be discarded.

Cooking times

All recipes and cooking times are based on microwave ovens with a power level on high of 680 watts.

If using a 500-watt oven, allow 15 seconds extra for every minute of cooking.

The following cooking times are a guide only and depend on the thickness of fish and the cooking method.

Fish	Total Cooking Time	Power Level
Whole fish	8-12 min/500 g	Medium-High
Fillets	5-11 min/500 g	High
Steaks	4-7 min/500 g	High
Shellfish (out of shell)	3½-7 min/500 g	High

If using frozen fish, microwave on defrost 3-5 minutes/500 g, stand for 2 minutes, and cook as directed in recipe.

Removal of fish odour

To remove any fish odours from the microwave oven, place a cup containing ¼ cup water and ¼ cup lemon juice or vinegar in the oven and bring to the boil. Microwave on medium 2-3 minutes. Wipe oven out with a damp cloth.

Recipes

Generally, individual fish species have not been mentioned in the recipes. This allows for maximum flexibility according to seasonal availability and preferred price range. For a guide to which species are suitable, please refer to the chart on p. 15.

WEIGHTS AND MEASURES

New Zealand standard kitchen measurements have been used for all recipes.

| 1 teaspoon | 5 ml | 1 cup | 250 ml |
| 1 tablespoon | 15 ml | 4 cups | 1 litre |

Abbreviations

tsp	teaspoon	g	gram
Tbsp	tablespoon	cm	centimetre
dsp	dessertspoon	°C	degrees Celsius

Metric Conversions

Grams	Ounces	Grams	Ounces
30	1	185	6
60	2	220	7
90	3	250	8 (½lb)
125	4 (¼lb)	375	12 (¾lb)
155	5	500	16 (1lb)

Oven Temperatures									
°C	100	120	140	150	160	180	190	200	220	230	250
°F	200	250	275	300	325	350	375	400	425	450	475

Centimetres	Inches	Centimetres	Inches
2.5	1	20	8
5	2	23	9
18	7	25	10

Symbols

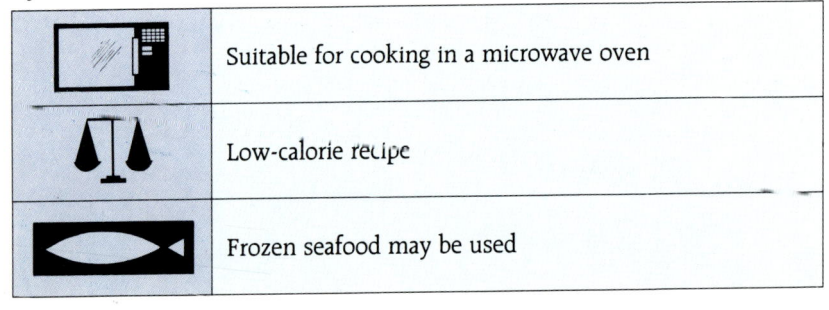

🔲	Suitable for cooking in a microwave oven
⚖	Low-calorie recipe
🐟	Frozen seafood may be used

HORS-D'OEUVRE

Fish Pâté

Makes 1½ cups

250 g delicate-textured, skinless, boneless fish
125 g cream cheese
1 tsp lemon juice
¼ tsp Worcestershire sauce
salt and pepper to taste

1. Poach and flake fish or foil-bake and flake.

2. Place fish, cream cheese, lemon juice and Worcestershire sauce in a food processor or blender and blend until mixture is thick and smooth. Season to taste with salt and pepper.

3. Spoon into a suitable container, cover with melted butter to seal if desired. Store in refrigerator for up to 3 days.

Serve on crackers, toast triangles or French bread.

Variations

1. *Smoked Fish Pâté*. Replace fish with 250 g hot- or cold-smoked fish, skinned and boned. If fish is cold-smoked, foil-bake at 180°C for 20-25 minutes.

2. *Oyster Pâté* (for raw oyster fans!). In step 2, replace fish with 12 oysters, chopped, and add 1 gherkin, roughly chopped.

Crab Pâté

Makes 1 cup

200 g crab meat
100 g unsalted butter
1 Tbsp finely chopped onion
pinch cayenne pepper

1. Melt butter in a saucepan, add onion, crab meat, cayenne pepper and toss over a low heat until crab is completely coated in butter.

2. Transfer to a ramekin or pâté dish and refrigerate.

Garnish with watercress and serve with crackers, toast or crusty French bread.

Hors-d'oeuvre

Pâté Parcels

Makes 20 parcels

1 cup smoked fish pâté (see p.51)
1 Tbsp onion, finely chopped (optional)
¼ tsp curry powder (optional)
400 g flaky pastry
1 egg, beaten

1. If using onion or curry powder, blend these into the pâté mixture.
2. Roll out pastry and cut into 8-cm diameter circles.
3. Brush beaten egg around edges of circles.
4. Place a small teaspoon of pâté in centre of each pastry circle. Bring the 2 edges of pastry up to join on top of pâté and seal edges.
5. Brush pastry parcels with beaten egg then place on a greased oven tray.
6. Bake at 220°C for 10-12 minutes.

Smoked Oyster Mousse

Serves 4

100 g smoked oysters or smoked mussels, drained
2 Tbsp onion, chopped
1½ tsp butter
4 tsp lemon juice
1 Tbsp tomato paste or sauce
125 g cream cheese
2 tsp gelatine
1 Tbsp boiling water
¼ cup cream
1 egg white

1. In a frypan, melt butter and sauté onion until soft.
2. Place sautéed onion, oysters or mussels, lemon juice, and tomato paste or sauce in a food processor or blender and process until the mixture forms a smooth purée. Add cream cheese and process to combine.
3. If a food processor or blender is not available, push oysters or mussels through a sieve and beat into the onion, lemon juice, tomato paste or sauce and cream cheese.
4. Dissolve gelatine in boiling water and combine with cream cheese mixture.
5. Whip cream until soft peaks form. Beat egg white until stiff. Fold cream into cream cheese mixture, then fold in egg white.
6. Pour mixture into a greased mould, smoothing the top. Chill until set, then unmould onto a serving plate.

Garnish if desired, with slices of cucumber and fresh parsley. Serve with crackers or thin slices of toast.

Hors-d'oeuvre

Pâté Parcels

Fluffy Oyster Balls
Makes 24

24 oysters
salt and pepper to taste
2 eggs, separated
2 Tbsp oyster juice
3 Tbsp cornflour
flour for coating
oil for deep frying
24 thin lemon slices (optional)

1. Strain oysters, remove any pieces of shell, reserve juice.
2. Add salt to egg whites and beat until stiff.
3. Add pepper and oyster juice to egg yolks, beat until light and creamy.
4. Fold cornflour into beaten yolks, then fold in egg whites.
5. Using a skewer, dip each oyster in flour and then in batter. Deep fry in hot oil at approximately 190°C until crisp and golden, about 3 minutes.
6. Drain and keep hot until all the oysters are cooked.
7. If desired, fold a lemon slice around each oyster ball and secure at one side with a toothpick.

Hors-d'oeuvre

Taramasalata

Makes 1½ cups

- 200 g red or blue cod smoked roe
- 1 clove garlic, crushed
- 2 Tbsp lemon juice
- 3 Tbsp olive oil
- 4 Tbsp cold water
- 1 cup fresh breadcrumbs

1. Skin smoked roe.

2. Place smoked roe, crushed garlic, lemon juice, olive oil, water and breadcrumbs in a food processor or blender and mix until a thick, smooth paste is formed.

3. Place in a small bowl, cover and chill.

Garnish with chopped parsley and lemon slices, and serve with slices of thin toast or crusty bread.

Fisharettes

Makes 30 rolls

- 100 g smoked fish (canned or fresh)
- 3 Tbsp butter
- 3 Tbsp flour
- ¼ tsp salt
- grind of black pepper
- 1 cup milk
- ½ tsp Worcestershire sauce
- ¼ cup grated cheese
- 1 tsp lemon juice
- 1 tsp chopped parsley
- fresh square loaf of thinly sliced bread, buttered

1. Drain and flake the canned smoked fish, or poach and flake fresh smoked fish, removing skin and bones.

2. To make sauce, melt butter, add flour and seasonings. Cook until bubbling.

3. Gradually stir in milk and cook 2-3 minutes until thickened.

4. Add Worcestershire sauce, cheese, lemon juice, parsley and fish. Mix well. Cool.

5. Place bread, buttered side down, on board and spread with fish mixture. Roll each slice up.

6. Secure with a toothpick and either grill over a barbecue or under a preheated grill for 2-3 minutes, each side, until browned; or wrap in foil (no need to use toothpicks), place on top of hot coals or in oven heated to 150°C, and heat through 10-15 minutes.

Crispy Seafood Surprises

Makes 36 triangles

- 200 g skinless, boneless fish, diced into 1-cm cubes
- 100 g mussel meats, finely chopped
- 2 Tbsp butter
- 3 spring onions or 1 small onion, finely chopped
- 3 Tbsp flour
- ½ cup milk
- ½ tsp dried basil
- salt to taste
- 1 egg, lightly beaten
- 1 tsp lemon juice
- freshly grated nutmeg
- freshly ground black pepper
- 200 g packet phyllo pastry
- ½ cup melted butter

1. Melt butter in a saucepan, sauté spring onions or onion until soft, approximately 2-3 minutes.

2. Add flour and cook 1-2 minutes until frothy.

3. Gradually stir in milk and heat until boiling, then add basil and fish.

4. Simmer 3-4 minutes until sauce is smooth and thickened. Season to taste with salt.

5. Stir in mussel meats, egg, lemon juice, nutmeg and pepper to taste. Allow to cool.

6. Cut sheets of pastry into widthwise strips 4 cm wide. Brush 1 strip with melted butter. Place a teaspoonful of filling on bottom left hand corner of strip. Fold bottom right hand corner over filling to form a triangle. Then fold triangle up, then to the right and continue folding, keeping triangle shape with each fold.

7. Place triangle, seam side down, on a greased tray. Repeat with remaining strips and filling.

8. Brush completed triangles with melted butter and bake at 200°C until golden brown, approximately 10-15 minutes.

Serve warm.

Hors-d'oeuvre

Tomatoes Stuffed with Smoked Oysters
Makes 24

100 g smoked oysters or smoked mussels, finely chopped
12 small tomatoes
salt and pepper
1 hard-boiled egg, finely chopped
¼ cup peeled, seeded and diced cucumber

½ tsp capers, chopped
½ tsp chopped chives
1 tsp French mustard
1 tsp lemon juice
1 Tbsp oil
salt and pepper to taste

1. Cut tops off tomatoes and carefully remove inside of each tomato with a spoon.

2. Place tomatoes upside down on a rack and leave to drain for 20 minutes.

3. Season inside of each tomato with salt and pepper.

4. Combine oysters, egg, cucumber, capers and chives.

5. Place mustard, lemon juice, oil and salt and pepper to taste in a screw-top jar and shake well.

6. Combine oyster and oil mixtures. Spoon into prepared tomatoes. Chill.

Mussel Toppings

Ideal for mussels on the half shell or mussel meats on a serving plate. Choose from the toppings below, then cook:

- raw mussels — grill 3-4 minutes, microwave 1-2 minutes
- cooked mussels — grill 2-3 minutes, microwave 1 minute
- frozen mussels — grill 5-6 minutes, microwave 2-3 minutes

Quantities are sufficient for 8-10 mussels. Serve as hors-d'oeuvre, or for lunch or dinner with bread and a salad.

Herb and Tomato
Combine 3 skinned and finely chopped tomatoes with ½ tsp dried sweet basil and a grind of black pepper. Allow 1 tsp mixture for each mussel.

Cheese and Bacon
Top each mussel with 2 tsp finely grated cheese and a pinch of bacon stock.

Garlic Butter
Soften 50 g butter and combine with 2 peeled and crushed cloves garlic. Spread over each mussel.

Spicy Peanut
Combine 3 Tbsp peanut butter with 1 Tbsp coconut cream and ¼ tsp chilli powder. Spread over each mussel.

Lemon Sauce
Combine ¼ cup sour cream, ½-1 tsp lemon juice, 1 peeled and crushed clove garlic and a grind of black pepper. Spoon over each mussel.

Crunchy Fish Won Tons

Makes 36 won tons

400 g skinless, boneless fish, cut into 1-cm cubes
2 Tbsp oil
¼ cup chopped spring onions
1 Tbsp soy sauce
1 Tbsp sherry
2 tsp oyster sauce* (optional)
1 tsp brown sugar
1 clove garlic, crushed
1 tsp grated fresh root ginger
salt and pepper to taste
1 tsp cornflour
2 tsp water
1 tsp sesame oil (optional)
36 won ton wrappers
oil for deep frying

1. Fry spring onions in oil, over a high heat, until soft — 2-3 minutes.
2. Remove from heat and add fish, soy sauce, sherry, oyster sauce, brown sugar, garlic, and ginger. Mix thoroughly and season to taste.
3. Return to a medium heat and stir until boiling.
4. Blend cornflour, water and sesame oil. Gradually stir this into fish mixture and cook gently until sauce is thickened. Remove from heat and cool.
5. Moisten edges of 1 won ton wrapper and place a heaped teaspoon of filling in centre of wrapper. To form a triangle, bring opposite points of the square wrapper together — they will not quite join in the centre. Press the side corners together to join.
6. Deep fry in hot oil until golden brown and crisp, approximately 1 minute. Drain well on absorbent paper.

Serve hot with Sweet and Sour Sauce (see Sauces).

*Oyster sauce may be purchased from oriental food merchants.

Hors-d'oeuvre

Simple Smoked Salmon

boneless smoked salmon fillets
butter, softened
brown bread
lemon wedges (optional)
black pepper (optional)

Garnish
parsley sprigs
lemon wedges or slices

1. Holding a very sharp knife on an angle, slice smoked salmon towards the skin to obtain wafer-thin slices. (If you find that the salmon is difficult to slice thinly and falls apart, chill it thoroughly or place it in the freezer for approximately 30 minutes prior to slicing.)

2. Lightly butter bread. Remove crusts and cut into triangles.

3. Place salmon slices on buttered bread. If desired, squeeze lemon juice over salmon and sprinkle with pepper.

Serve on a lettuce-lined platter garnished with parsley sprigs and lemon wedges or slices.

Smoked Seafood Platter

With the wide variety of smoked seafood available, a smoked seafood platter can be very attractive and easy to prepare. It is often an excellent conversation piece, too.

Serving suggestions

1. Some smoked seafoods such as octopus, oysters, eel, mussels, and squid may be served unaccompanied or may be presented on a lettuce leaf lined platter, garnished with lemon slices and sprigs of fresh herbs. Toothpicks may be provided.

2. Smoked fish such as salmon, tuna, hake, red cod, ling, hoki and roe (cod or groper) is best presented sliced thinly and served on crackers, French bread or wholemeal bread. Different base spreads may be used instead of butter, such as horseradish with marlin or mayonnaise with salmon. Suitable topping ideas are slices of green or red pepper, olives, gherkins, tomato, cucumber and egg.

3. The platter may include a smoked fish pâté and/or taramasalata which are served with crackers, slices of thin toast or crusty bread.

Hors-d'oeuvre

Simple Smoked Salmon

Marinated Seafood Platter

Marinated seafoods such as mussels, squid, octopus are best eaten in their marinated state. They may be served in lettuce leaf lined bowls, garnished with sprigs of parsley and accompanied by toothpicks.

SOUPS

White Fish Stock
Makes about 3 cups

500 g bones, trimmings and heads of white fish
1 cup sliced onion
12 parsley stems
2 Tbsp lemon juice
½ tsp salt
3½ cups water
½ cup dry white wine

1. Combine fish, onion, parsley, lemon juice and salt in a heavy-based saucepan. Cover and steam mixture over a moderately high heat for 5 minutes.

2. Add water and wine and bring to the boil. Skim froth off as it rises to the surface.

3. Simmer stock for 25 minutes.

4. Strain stock through a fine sieve into a bowl, pressing hard on the solids. Cool.

This is a simple, delicious stock which may be used as the basis for many soups. It may be frozen.

Oriental Fish Soup
Serves 4

400 g medium- to firm-textured, skinless, boneless fish fillets
3 Tbsp butter
2 onions, finely chopped
1 clove garlic, crushed
1 dsp finely chopped root ginger
1 green pepper, finely chopped
150 g mushrooms, thinly sliced
1 litre water or fish stock
1 Tbsp lemon juice
½ tsp brown sugar
1 tsp soy sauce
2-3 Tbsp sherry
salt and pepper to taste

1. Cut fish into 2-cm cubes.

2. Melt butter in a saucepan, sauté onions, garlic, ginger and green pepper until onion is soft.

3. Add mushrooms and cook 1-2 minutes.

4. Add cubed fish, water or fish stock, lemon juice, brown sugar, soy sauce and sherry. Cook gently 5-7 minutes. Season to taste.

Serve garnished with a sprinkling of finely chopped spring onions.

Bouillabaisse-style Soup

Serves 4-6

- 1.25 kg medium-textured, skinless, boneless fish e.g. tarakihi, gurnard, blue cod
- 6 shellfish e.g. mussels, tuatuas, pipis
- 100 ml oil
- 1 small onion, chopped
- 2 cloves garlic, crushed
- 2 tomatoes, peeled, seeded and chopped
- ½ leek, chopped
- 1 sprig fennel
- 1 sprig thyme
- 1 bay leaf
- 1 strip orange peel
- 1.25 litres boiling water
- 2 pinches saffron (optional)
- salt and pepper to taste

1. Cut fish into 3-cm cubes.

2. Heat oil in a large saucepan. Add onion, garlic, tomatoes, leek, fennel, thyme, bay leaf and orange peel. Gently sauté 8 minutes, mixing well.

3. Stir in boiling water and boil 5 minutes: this is to allow the oil and water to form an emulsion, giving a smooth sauce.

4. Add cubed fish and simmer 10 minutes.

5. Add saffron, if desired, and season to taste. Add whole shellfish and simmer until these open 1-2 cm. Discard those shellfish that do not open.

Serve in large soup bowls.

Fish and Asparagus Soup

Serves 4-6

- 500 g medium- to firm-textured, skinless, boneless fish fillets
- 1 Tbsp butter
- 1 onion, chopped
- 2 rashers bacon, chopped
- 1 Tbsp flour
- ½ cup milk
- ½ cup water
- 1 x 455 g can asparagus pieces

1. Cut fish into 2-cm cubes.

2. Melt butter in a saucepan. Add onion and bacon and cook 3-4 minutes.

3. Blend in flour and cook 1-2 minutes until frothy.

4. Gradually stir in milk, water and undrained can of asparagus pieces. Bring to the boil.

5. Add cubed fish and simmer until fish is cooked.

Top with whipped cream and serve with crusty fresh bread.

Oyster and Lemon Soup

Serves 4

12 oysters, finely chopped
2 Tbsp butter
3 spring onions, finely chopped
2 Tbsp flour
2 cups chicken stock or 2 tsp chicken stock powder dissolved in 2 cups water

1 cup milk
1 Tbsp lemon juice
pinch ground mace or nutmeg
salt and pepper to taste

1. Heat butter in a saucepan and gently cook spring onions 2-3 minutes.
2. Add flour and cook 2 minutes until foaming.
3. Stir in chicken stock and milk and cook until mixture boils and thickens. Simmer 3-4 minutes.
4. Blend in oysters and lemon juice.
5. Adjust seasonings and reheat but do not boil.

Garnish, if desired, with sour cream and serve with fresh crusty bread.

Shellfish Cauldron

Serves 4

500 g medium- to firm-textured, skinless, boneless fish fillets
6-8 scallops
6 mussel meats, roughly chopped
6 oysters
1 x 100 g can shrimps
¼ cup cooking oil
1 onion, chopped

1 stalk celery, sliced
3 tomatoes, peeled and roughly chopped
1 Tbsp chopped parsley
1 bay leaf
1¼ cups water or fish stock
350 ml dry white wine
salt and pepper to taste

1. Cut fish into 2-cm cubes.
2. Heat oil in a large saucepan. Add onion and celery and cook until tender.
3. Add fish, tomatoes, parsley, bay leaf and water or fish stock. Cook gently for 10 minutes. Don't boil rapidly at any stage as this causes the fish to break up.
4. Add scallops and cook a further 10 minutes. Remove bay leaf.
5. Add mussels, oysters, shrimps and wine. Cook gently 2-3 minutes but do not boil as mixture may curdle. Season to taste with salt and pepper.

Serve with French bread or bread rolls.

Oyster and Lemon Soup

Jiffy Mussel Chowder

Serves 4

9 mussel meats
1 packet leek and potato soup
1 cup water
1 x 310 g can whole kernel sweet corn, drained
1 cup frozen peas
1 Tbsp mayonnaise
1 cup milk
salt and pepper to taste

1. Chop finely or mince 3 mussels. Chop remaining 6 mussels roughly.

2. In a saucepan, mix soup to a paste with a little of the water. Add remaining water and minced mussels. Cook until thickened, stirring constantly.

3. Stir in corn, peas, mayonnaise and milk. Heat to boiling.

4. Add roughly chopped mussels and heat for 2-3 minutes, without boiling. Season to taste.

Serve with melba toast or bread rolls.

Soups

Jo's Spanish Soup

Serves 4

750 g medium- to firm-textured, skinless, boneless fish fillets
2 Tbsp oil
2 onions, finely chopped
2 cloves garlic, crushed
½ cup tomato purée
¼ tsp dried thyme
¼ tsp dried basil
1 Tbsp chopped parsley
2 bay leaves
1 tsp turmeric
½ cup white wine
2½-3 cups water
1 tsp chicken stock powder
3 Tbsp lemon juice
salt and pepper to taste

1. Cut fish into 2-cm cubes.

2. Heat oil in a large saucepan. Add onions and garlic and cook until softened.

3. Add tomato purée, thyme, basil, parsley, bay leaves and turmeric and cook 5 minutes.

4. Add wine, water, chicken stock and lemon juice. Simmer 10 minutes.

5. Stir in cubed fish and continue to simmer gently for a further 15 minutes. Season to taste.

Serve in large soup bowls with crusty fresh bread.

Fish Chowder

Serves 4-6

300 g delicate-textured, skinless, boneless fish fillets
300 g potatoes, peeled and chopped
3 cups boiling water
½ tsp salt
1 stick celery, finely chopped
salt and pepper to taste

1. Cut fish into 2-cm cubes.

2. Cook prepared potatoes in boiling salted water, until soft, approximately 10 minutes.

3. Add diced fish and finely chopped celery and cook a further 5 minutes. Remove from heat.

4. Process in food processor or blender, or push through sieve until smooth.

5. Reheat.

Garnish, if desired, with sour cream.

Country Chowder

Serves 4-6

- 300 g hot- or cold-smoked fish, skinned and boned
- 4 Tbsp butter
- 2 medium potatoes, finely chopped
- 1 onion, finely chopped
- 3 Tbsp flour
- 3 cups milk
- ¾ cup assorted vegetables, e.g. celery, green peppers (finely chopped), peas, beans (fresh, frozen or canned)
- 1 x 310 g can whole kernel corn, undrained
- salt and pepper to taste

1. Cut fish into 2-cm cubes.
2. Melt butter in a large saucepan, sauté potatoes and onion 10 minutes until soft.
3. Add flour and cook 2 minutes.
4. Gradually stir in milk and simmer until thickened.
5. Add cubed fish and cook 2-3 minutes.
6. Add mixed vegetables and corn and simmer 5 minutes. Season to taste with salt and pepper.

Serve with crusty bread.

Country Chowder

Soups

Seafood Medley Soup
Serves 4

- 400 g mixed shellfish, removed from shell e.g. mussels, pipis, cockles
- 100 g medium- to firm-textured, skinless, boneless fish fillets
- 2 Tbsp butter
- 1 onion, sliced
- 2 cloves garlic, crushed
- 2 large tomatoes, peeled, seeded and chopped or 2 Tbsp tomato paste
- 1 Tbsp finely chopped parsley
- 1 sprig rosemary, finely chopped
- 1 tsp grated lemon rind
- 1 Tbsp flour
- 2 cups water
- 1 tsp sugar
- dash tabasco sauce
- salt and pepper to taste

1. Slice large shellfish and cut fish into 2-cm cubes.
2. Melt butter in a large saucepan, sauté onion and garlic until onion softens.
3. Add tomatoes or tomato paste, parsley, rosemary and lemon rind. Cook 3-4 minutes. Stir in flour.
4. Add water, sugar and tabasco sauce. Bring to the boil and simmer 5 minutes.
5. Add shellfish and fish. Reheat until seafood is cooked, but do not boil. Season to taste.

Serve in individual bowls with a swirl of cream.

Variations

1. *Seafood and Pasta Soup.* In step 4, add ½ cup uncooked pasta e.g. pasta shells, and ½ cup water and simmer until pasta is cooked.

2. For a richer soup — in step 5, add 2 Tbsp dry white wine and ¼ cup cream.

Shellfish Soup
Serves 4

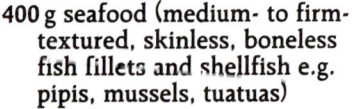

- 400 g seafood (medium- to firm-textured, skinless, boneless fish fillets and shellfish e.g. pipis, mussels, tuatuas)
- 2 Tbsp butter
- 1 onion, finely chopped
- ½ tsp curry powder
- 1 Tbsp flour
- ½ cup tomato purée
- 300 ml milk
- 200 ml water
- 1 Tbsp white wine or lemon juice
- ½ tsp sugar
- salt and pepper to taste

1. Cut fish into 2-cm cubes. Steam open shellfish (see p. 38) and remove meat from shells. Finely chop or mince shellfish meats.

2. Melt butter in a saucepan and cook onion and curry powder for 2 minutes.

3. Stir in flour and cook 1 minute, then blend in tomato purée.

4. Gradually stir in milk and heat until boiling.

5. Stir in water and bring to boil again.

6. Add seafood and heat gently until fish is cooked. Don't overcook or the shellfish will toughen.

7. Stir in wine or lemon juice and season to taste with sugar, salt and pepper. Do not boil again as the soup may curdle.

Serve with bread rolls.

Creamy Seafood Soup

Serves 6

- 15 mussels
- 12 oysters, removed from shell
- ½ cup wine
- bouquet garni (onion, parsley, thyme)
- 3 Tbsp butter
- 2 onions, chopped
- 3 Tbsp flour
- 3 cups fish stock
- 1 cup milk
- 1 cup cream
- salt and pepper to taste

1. Put wine, bouquet garni and mussels in a large saucepan. Cover and steam until the mussels open. Discard mussels that do not open.

2. Strain and reserve wine and mussel liquor.

3. Put aside 6 of the cooked mussels, still in shells, to use as a garnish. Remove mussel meats from the other 9 mussels. Finely chop or mince 3 mussel meats. Roughly chop the remaining 6 mussel meats.

4. Melt butter in the same saucepan. Add chopped onion and cook until translucent.

5. Blend in flour and cook until frothy, then add minced mussel meats.

6. Measure wine and mussel liquor and add sufficient fish stock to make up 3½ cups liquid. Gradually stir this liquid and the milk into onion mixture 1 cup at a time, boiling between each addition.

7. Mix in cream, chopped mussels and oysters. Heat gently until the oysters are cooked. Add the 6 reserved opened mussels, still in shells, to soup. Heat through but do not boil. Season to taste with salt and pepper.

Serve in large soup bowls with an opened mussel in each bowl.

Soups

Mussel Chowder
Serves 6

- 12 large or 24 small fresh mussels, or 250 g mussel meats, cooked
- 500 g potatoes, peeled and finely chopped
- 3 cups boiling water
- salt to taste
- 1 tsp grated lemon rind
- 4 Tbsp cream
- freshly ground black pepper

1. If using fresh mussels, follow directions for cleaning and cooking (see p. 36). Remove meat from shells. Chop cooked meat finely or mince.
2. Cook chopped potatoes in boiling salted water until just tender.
3. Add chopped or minced mussels, lemon rind, cream and black pepper.
4. Simmer gently for 5 minutes, do not boil.

Mussel Chowder

Scallop and Fish Soup

Serves 4

100 g medium- to firm-textured, skinless, boneless fish fillets
6 to 8 scallops, sliced
2 Tbsp butter
100 g mushrooms, sliced
1 onion, finely sliced
2 cloves garlic, crushed

2 Tbsp flour
¼ cup dry white wine
600 ml milk
2 Tbsp cream or top milk
salt and pepper to taste

1. Cut fish into 2-cm cubes.
2. Melt butter in a saucepan. Add mushrooms, onion and garlic and cook until tender.
3. Add diced fish and cook 3-4 minutes.
4. Stir in flour and wine, mixed to a smooth paste.
5. Gradually stir in milk and simmer gently for 5 minutes.
6. Add scallops and simmer 1 minute.
7. Stir in cream and season to taste. Reheat without boiling.

Serve sprinkled with chopped parsley.

STARTERS AND ENTRÉES

Seviche
Serves 4

500 g scallops, cleaned
juice of 4 lemons or 8 limes
½ cup olive oil
1-2 cloves garlic, crushed
1 Tbsp finely chopped spring onions

1 Tbsp finely chopped green chillies
1 Tbsp finely chopped parsley
salt to taste

1. Place cleaned scallops and lemon or lime juice in a non-aluminium bowl.

2. Cover and chill overnight in refrigerator. (They will change from translucent to opaque.) Drain well.

3. Combine remaining ingredients and toss scallops in this dressing. Chill 1 hour.

Serve immediately on lettuce leaves.

Crumbed Squid Rings
Squid hood about 20 cm long serves 6 for an entrée

1 squid hood
1 raw kiwifruit (for marinating)
½ cup flour
1-2 eggs, beaten
½ tsp salt

freshly ground black pepper
1 cup dry breadcrumbs (for coating)
oil for cooking

1. Cut hood into rings and either blanch in boiling water 1 minute or marinate in kiwifruit to tenderise (see page 45).

2. Toss squid in flour to dry it, dip into beaten egg and seasonings, and then breadcrumbs. If time permits, lay on a cake rack or plate in refrigerator for at least 10 minutes to set the crumbs.

3. When ready to cook, heat enough oil to cover the bottom of a heavy-based frypan or electric frypan (180°C). Add coated rings and cook for approximately 15 seconds on each side, until golden brown.

4. Remove from oil and drain on absorbent paper.

Serve as an entrée with a seafood sauce (see Sauces) or with salads as a main course.

Pawpaw and Crab Entrée

Pawpaw and Crab Entrée

Serves 4

200 g crab meat
1 pawpaw*
1 Tbsp lemon juice

2 Tbsp mayonnaise
2 tsp mild chilli sauce
freshly ground black pepper

1. Halve, peel and deseed pawpaw. Cut each pawpaw half into 4 wedges.
2. Toss crab meat in lemon juice.
3. Mix together mayonnaise, chilli sauce and freshly ground black pepper.
4. Place 2 wedges of pawpaw together on 4 serving plates. Arrange a quarter of the crab meat over each serving. Spoon a little chilli mayonnaise on top.

Garnish with chopped chives and lemon slices.

*Pawpaw is also known as papaya.

Starters and Entrées

Standard Crepe Recipe

1 cup flour
3 eggs
1 cup milk

pinch salt
25 g butter, melted

1. Sift flour into a bowl.
2. Add lightly beaten eggs, milk and salt. Mix until batter is smooth.
3. Stir in melted butter.
4. Lightly grease and heat an 18-cm crepe (frying) pan.
5. Pour approximately 2 Tbsp batter into the pan. Cook till golden on 1 side then turn over and cook second side.
6. Continue until all batter has been used.

Stacked Seafood Crepes

Serves 4

300 g medium-textured, skinless, boneless fish fillets
1 Tbsp butter
1 stick celery, finely diced
1 small clove garlic, crushed
3 tomatoes, skinned and chopped
1 bay leaf
50 g mushrooms, sliced
¼ cup grated cheese
salt and pepper to taste

1. Cut fish into 1-cm cubes.

2. Heat butter in pan. Add celery and garlic and cook gently 3 minutes, until soft.

3. Add tomatoes, bay leaf and mushrooms and cook 3 minutes, stirring occasionally.

4. Mix in grated cheese, diced fish and seasonings. Remove from heat.

5. Lightly grease a 20-cm round baking dish. Place a crepe flat on the bottom of the dish, spread with 2 Tbsp filling, and continue alternately layering crepes with filling. Do not stack higher than 12 cm.

6. Cover crepe stack with foil and bake at 190°C for 15 minutes until hot throughout.

Serve cut into quarters with a salad.

Oyster and Spinach Crepes

Serves 9 as an entrée or 6 as a main course

12 oysters, chopped
200 g spinach
boiling water for blanching
2 Tbsp butter

2 Tbsp flour
¾ cup milk
salt and pepper to taste

1. Wash and trim spinach. Blanch in boiling water for 2 minutes. Drain, discarding liquid. Chop spinach finely and leave to drain thoroughly.
2. Melt butter in saucepan, stir in flour and cook gently 1-2 minutes.
3. Blend in milk, salt and pepper, stir well.
4. Cook gently until boiling and thickened.
5. Remove from heat and add cooked spinach and chopped oysters.
6. Place 2 Tbsp filling on each crepe and roll up.
7. Place filled crepes in a lightly greased baking dish.
8. Cover and bake at 200°C for 10-12 minutes. Remove cover for the last 2 minutes.

Serve garnished with lemon and tomato wedges.

Grilled Scallop Kebabs

Serves 4

500 g scallops (about 30)
3 Tbsp butter, melted
pepper to taste

8 rashers lean bacon
1 x 455 g can pineapple pieces
8 skewers

1. Combine butter and pepper. Dip scallops in this, lift out and refrigerate to solidify butter.
2. Trim rind from bacon, thread 1 end of each strip of bacon on a skewer, then a scallop and a pineapple piece. Bring bacon round scallop and pineapple piece and thread over skewer. Repeat until each skewer has 3 or 4 scallops partially enfolded in bacon.
3. Cook for about 8 minutes under a preheated grill, turning several times and brushing with butter if necessary.

Serve with Hollandaise Sauce (see Sauces).

Starters and Entrées

Smoked Fish Kebabs
Serves 4

450 g hot- or cold-smoked fish, skinned and boned
8 rashers lean, rindless bacon
selection of button mushrooms, pineapple pieces, tomato or onion segments, banana pieces (1.5 cm in length) dipped in lemon juice, or pieces of red or green pepper

2 Tbsp cooking oil
salt and pepper to taste
8 skewers

1. Cut fish into 1.5-cm cubes.
2. Cut bacon into strips and wrap around each piece of fish.
3. Combine fruit and vegetable pieces, oil and seasonings in a bowl and toss.
4. Thread wrapped fish onto skewers with prepared fruit and vegetables.
5. Place kebabs under a preheated grill or on a barbecue.
6. Grill 8-10 minutes, turning several times.

Serve with French bread or on a bed of rice.

Smoked Fish Kebabs

Cream-baked Scallops

Serves 4 as an entrée or 2 as a main course

12 scallops (about 200 g)
25 g butter
½ cup soft white breadcrumbs
½ cup cream

salt and pepper to taste
squeeze lemon juice
4 scallop shells or ramekins

1. Melt butter in a small frypan, then place a teaspoonful in each of the 4 shells or ramekins.
2. Add breadcrumbs to remaining butter and cook until they become slightly crisp and golden.
3. Place 3 scallops in each shell.
4. Combine cream, salt and pepper and lemon juice and pour a quarter of the cream mixture in each shell.
5. Top with a sprinkling of buttered crumbs.
6. Place shells in an ovenproof dish and bake at 200°C for about 8 minutes.

Serve with toast, wholemeal bread or rolls.

Oyster Kilpatrick

Serves 3-4 as an entrée or 2 as a main course

12 oysters
1 tsp Worcestershire sauce
¼ tsp salt

¼ tsp pepper
2 rashers bacon, cut into thin strips

1. Open oysters and leave them on the half shell or alternatively, place several oysters in scallop shells or ramekins.
2. Season each oyster with a drop of Worcestershire sauce, a pinch of salt and a grind of pepper.
3. Cover oysters with strips of thinly cut bacon.
4. Cook for 5 minutes at 200°C or cook under a preheated grill for 3 minutes.

Serve garnished with lemon wedges and parsley.

Starters and Entrées

Marinade Bacchus

Serves 6 as an entrée or 3 as a main course

500 g skinless, boneless, medium-textured fish fillets, cubed into 1-cm pieces
juice of 6 lemons and 2 oranges, to give 2 cups juice in total
½ cup dry white wine
½ small onion, finely chopped

1. Place all ingredients in a plastic bag or bowl (not aluminium), mix thoroughly. Place in refrigerator overnight or for 8 hours, until flesh is opaque throughout.
2. When ready to use, drain off marinade and coat with a seafood sauce (see Sauces).

Serve with salad and rolls or garlic bread.

Herb Marinated Mussels

Serves 4 as an entrée or 2-3 as a main course

20 mussels (fresh steam-opened or thawed frozen)
½ cup lemon juice
1 cup cider vinegar
salt and pepper to taste
1 small onion, chopped
1 Tbsp chopped fresh parsley
1 Tbsp chopped fresh marjoram

1. Place all ingredients in a bowl (not aluminium) and mix well.
2. Leave for at least 1 hour in refrigerator. Stir occasionally. Use within 2 days.
3. Drain and serve.

Serve as a cocktail snack or entrée. Serve with a green salad and French bread as a main course.

Pink and White Terrine

Serves 4 5

250 g scallops
Basic Mixture
125 g delicate-textured, skinless, boneless fish fillets
1 egg
200 ml cream
1 Tbsp sour cream

salt and pepper to taste
(white flesh of scallops)
Crab Meat Layer
4 crab or seafood sticks, roughly chopped
Pink Layer
2 Tbsp beaten egg

3 Tbsp cream
(scallop roes)
Terrine Garnish
2 crab or seafood sticks
1 small avocado, peeled and cut into strips
1½ tsp chopped fresh dill (optional)

1. Separate pink roes from white flesh of scallops.

Basic Mixture

2. Place white flesh of scallops and fish fillets in a food processor or blender. Process until a fairly smooth paste is formed.

3. Add egg and process to combine ingredients. Chill the mixture for 1 hour.

4. Add cream, sour cream, salt and pepper to taste and process again. Remove ½ cup of the mixture and set aside.

Crab Meat Layer

5. Add chopped crab to the mixture in food processor. Process until mixture forms a smooth paste. Season to taste.

6. Remove from food processor bowl and set aside.

Pink Layer

7. Place ½ cup reserved basic mixture and scallop roes into food processor.

8. Add egg and cream and process until a smooth paste is formed. Season to taste.

9. Line a terrine or loaf tin with foil. Grease foil.

10. Place half the crab mixture in the terrine or loaf tin and spread with half the pink mixture.

11. Place crab or seafood sticks and avocado strips over pink layer and, if desired, sprinkle with chopped dill.

12. Spread with remaining pink mixture, then finish with other half of crab mixture. Cover top with a piece of greased foil.

13. Place in a baking dish and pour in enough hot water to come halfway up the side of the terrine dish. Cook at 180°C for 50-60 minutes or until terrine is set. Chill for a few hours.

Garnish with fresh herbs and serve cold, cut into slices. Accompany with Herb Mayonnaise (see Sauces).

Starters and Entrées

Pain de Poisson

Spicy Fish

Serves 6 as an entrée or 3-4 as a main course

> **500 g medium- to firm-textured, skinless, boneless fish fillets**
> **1 tsp curry powder**
> **¼ tsp salt**
>
> **25 g butter**
> **1 Tbsp cooking oil**

1. Cut fish into 2-cm cubes and sprinkle with curry powder and salt.

2. Heat butter and oil in pan. Sauté fish cubes 3-5 minutes (if frozen, allow extra 3 minutes).

3. Remove from pan and drain on absorbent paper.

Serve as an entrée or main course on a bed of rice.

Pain de Poisson
Serves 6-8

- 500 g delicate- to medium-textured, skinless, boneless fish fillets
- 6 mussel meats
- 3 egg whites
- 500 ml cream
- salt and freshly ground black pepper to taste
- pinch cayenne pepper
- 170 g fresh white breadcrumbs
- 3 egg yolks
- 4 Tbsp chopped parsley
- 2 Tbsp chopped tarragon and chives
- sprigs of fresh tarragon
- 10 rashers streaky bacon

1. In a food processor, mince the fish fillets in batches with 2 of the egg whites.

2. In a bowl, blend minced fish with 300 ml of the cream, salt, pepper and cayenne pepper. Place in refrigerator to thicken slightly.

3. Mince mussels finely in food processor.

4. In a bowl, mix breadcrumbs and chopped herbs with mussels, egg yolks and remaining cream. Check seasonings.

5. Place tarragon sprigs in the bottom of a 2-litre terrine. Line terrine with bacon, leaving enough to be folded over top of terrine.

6. Spread two-thirds of the fish mixture around base and sides of terrine. Brush with a little egg white.

7. Cover with the mussel mixture then brush with egg white.

8. Top with remaining fish mixture. Fold bacon over top.

9. Cover with damp greaseproof paper then foil. Stand terrine in a roasting pan of hot water. Cook at 150°C for 1-1½ hours. Test by pressing a skewer into the centre; hold there 5 seconds. It should be hot when held against your wrist. The top of the terrine should be firm. Turn out onto a serving plate.

Serve warm with Hollandaise Sauce (see Sauces) or cold with toast.

LIGHT MEALS

Salmon Loaf

Serves 4

250 g cooked and flaked salmon (salmon offcuts are ideal)
2 eggs
½ cup milk
½ cup dried breadcrumbs
1 Tbsp finely chopped onion
1 x 310 g can creamed corn
1 Tbsp chopped parsley
salt and pepper to taste

1. Beat eggs. Add milk, breadcrumbs, onion, corn, parsley and salmon and mix thoroughly. Season to taste with salt and pepper.
2. Pack mixture lightly into a greased loaf tin.
3. Cook at 180°C for 40-45 minutes or until firm.

Cut in slices and serve with a green salad.

Variation

1. *Smoked Salmon Loaf.* Replace salmon with 250 g flaked smoked salmon.

Shellfish Quiche

Serves 4-6

24 shellfish e.g. oysters, tuatuas, pipis
200 g flaky pastry
1 Tbsp butter
1 onion, finely chopped
2 rashers bacon, chopped
250 g sour cream
2 eggs, beaten
salt and pepper to taste

1. Roll out pastry and line base and sides of a 20-cm quiche dish. Place in refrigerator while preparing filling.
2. Melt butter in pan, gently cook chopped onion and bacon 3 minutes.
3. Roughly chop 12 of the shellfish, leaving remaining 12 whole.
4. Combine cooked onion and bacon mixture with shellfish, sour cream, beaten eggs and seasonings to taste. Mix well.
5. Pour into prepared pastry case and bake at 200°C for 10 minutes, then reduce temperature to 180°C and bake a further 25-30 minutes until filling is set.

Serve hot or cold with a tossed salad and crusty bread.

Kedgeree

Serves 3-4

200 g hot- or cold-smoked fish
1 cup long grain rice
50 g butter
2 Tbsp oil
1 onion, finely chopped
2 tsp curry powder
1 cup corn kernels — frozen, canned or fresh
1 cup peas — frozen, canned or fresh
3 hard-boiled eggs, chopped
salt and pepper to taste

1. If fish is cold-smoked, foil-bake at 180°C for 20-25 minutes.
2. Flake fish, removing skin and bones.
3. Cook rice in boiling salted water until tender. Drain.
4. Melt butter and oil in a large frypan or saucepan and sauté chopped onion and flaked fish 2-3 minutes.
5. Add curry powder, corn, peas, drained rice and chopped hard-boiled eggs.
6. Combine thoroughly, heat through. Season to taste and serve immediately.

Serve unaccompanied.

Kedgeree

Light Meals

Salmon-Cheese Puff
Serves 4

250 g cooked and flaked salmon (salmon offcuts are ideal)
1 cup milk
1 Tbsp lemon juice
2 Tbsp chopped parsley
½ tsp dry mustard
salt to taste
3 cups soft breadcrumbs
1 cup grated tasty cheese
3 eggs, separated

1. Combine fish, milk, lemon juice, parsley, mustard, salt, breadcrumbs, cheese and egg yolks.

2. Beat egg whites until stiff and fold into fish mixture.

3. Pour into a greased ovenware dish and bake at 180°C for 30-40 minutes or until firm.

Serve with a tossed salad.

Variations

1. *Smoked Salmon-Cheese Puff.* Replace salmon with 250 g flaked smoked salmon.

2. *Fish-Cheese Puff.* Replace salmon with a 1 x 310 g can fish, e.g. tuna, mackerel, drained and flaked.

Seafood Puff
Serves 4

1 x 310 g can fish, e.g. tuna, mackerel, drained and flaked
2½ cups soft breadcrumbs
½ cup milk
3 eggs, separated
grated rind of 1 lemon
1 Tbsp lemon juice
2 Tbsp chopped onion
salt to taste
grind black pepper

1. Combine 2 cups breadcrumbs with fish, milk, egg yolks, lemon rind and juice, onion and seasonings.

2. Beat egg whites until stiff and fold into fish mixture.

3. Pour into a greased ovenware dish and sprinkle with remaining ½ cup breadcrumbs.

4. Bake at 180°C for 30-40 minutes or until firm.

Serve with a salad.

Light Meals

Tasty Mussel Pie

Serves 4-6

- 12 fresh mussels or 250 g mussel meats, cooked, or 250 g marinated mussels, drained
- 200 g flaky pastry
- 3 eggs
- ½ cup cream or milk
- 1 onion, finely chopped
- ½ cup grated cheese
- juice of 1 lemon
- salt and pepper to taste

1. If using fresh mussels follow directions for cleaning and cooking (p. 36). Remove meat from shells. Mince or finely chop cooked or marinated mussels.

2. Roll out pastry and line base and sides of a 20-cm pie tin. If time permits, chill 30 minutes to prevent pastry shrinking.

3. Combine all other ingredients and mix well.

4. Pour into pastry case and bake at 180°C for 45 minutes or until filling is set and pastry golden.

Serve hot or cold with a salad and bread rolls.

Light Meals

Fish and Asparagus Flan
Serves 4-6

200 g skinless, boneless fish fillets, cut into 1-cm cubes
200 g flaky pastry
100 g asparagus, fresh or canned
½ cup cottage cheese
½ cup milk
2 eggs
salt and pepper to taste

1. Roll out pastry and line base and sides of a 20-cm flan or quiche dish. If time permits, chill 30 minutes to prevent pastry shrinking.
2. Spread cubed fish over pastry base.
3. If using fresh asparagus, blanch in boiling water, drain. Cut asparagus spears into 1.5-cm lengths. Sprinkle over fish.
4. Beat together cottage cheese, milk, eggs and salt and pepper to taste. Carefully pour this over fish and asparagus.
5. Bake at 200°C for 40 minutes or until pastry is golden and filling is set.

Serve hot or cold with a salad and French bread.

Variations
1. *Fish and Leek Flan.* Replace asparagus with 1 leek. Blanch leek as in step 3 and slice.
2. *Fish and Celery Flan.* Replace asparagus with ½ cup sliced celery.
3. *Fish and Spinach Flan.* Replace asparagus with 100 g spinach. Blanch spinach as in step 3 and slice.

Fish Soufflé
Serves 4

250 g delicate- to medium-textured fish
3 Tbsp butter
3 Tbsp flour
1 cup milk
1 Tbsp lemon juice
1 Tbsp chopped parsley
salt and pepper to taste
4 eggs, separated

1. Steam, poach, foil-bake or microwave fish until cooked.
2. Flake fish, removing skin and bones.
3. Melt butter in a saucepan, blend in flour and cook 1-2 minutes until bubbling.
4. Gradually stir in milk and heat until boiling.

Light Meals

5. Remove from heat and stir in lemon juice, parsley and salt and pepper to taste.

6. In separate bowls, beat egg yolks until thick and egg whites until stiff.

7. Fold yolks into sauce, then very gently fold in whites.

8. Pour mixture into a greased 15-20 cm soufflé dish and, to ensure even cooking, place in a pan of hot water.

9. Bake at 180°C for 45-55 minutes or until firm — gently insert the tip of a knife into centre of soufflé to test firmness.

Serve unaccompanied or with a green salad.

Seafood Fried Rice

Serves 4-6

400 g medium-textured, skinless, boneless fish fillets
6 mussels, finely chopped (optional)
2 rashers bacon, chopped
oil for cooking
2 eggs
salt and pepper to taste

1 tsp finely grated root ginger
2 cloves garlic, crushed
1 cup chopped spring onions
4 cups cooked long grain rice
1 cup frozen peas
2 tsp soy sauce

1. Cut fish into 2-cm cubes.

2. Cook bacon in a heavy-based frypan or wok until golden brown and crisp. Remove bacon from pan, and if necessary add extra oil to lightly grease pan.

3. Beat eggs together and season with salt and pepper.

4. Pour enough egg mixture into pre-greased pan to cover base in a thick layer. Cook until mixture starts to lift around edges, turn over and cook until set. Remove from pan and repeat as above until all the egg mixture has been used. Roll up like pancakes and cut into thin strips.

5. Heat approximately 1 Tbsp oil in the same pan. Add ginger, garlic, spring onions and fish and cook until onion softens.

6. Add rice and peas and cook, tossing, until rice is golden brown, approximately 5 minutes.

7. Add bacon, egg strips, soy sauce and, if desired, mussels. Cook, tossing again, until heated through.

Serve hot.

Light Meals

Open Crab Sandwiches

cooked, flaked crab meat	softened butter
thinly sliced wholemeal bread	mayonnaise
Sandwich Toppings	
lettuce leaves	tomato slices
cucumber slices	orange slices
black olives	hard-boiled eggs, quartered
pineapple rings	

1. Spread bread with butter or mayonnaise.

2. Using any combination of sandwich toppings, arrange the ingredients decoratively on bread slices.

3. Sprinkle with crab meat.

Serve with mayonnaise and lemon wedges.

Smoked Fish Roulade

Serves 4-6

500 g delicate- to medium-textured, hot- or cold-smoked fish	**Filling**
	¼ cup cottage cheese
	1 Tbsp lemon juice
60 g butter	¼ cup cream
⅓ cup flour	½ cup finely chopped parsley
¾ cup milk	½ cup grated cheese
4 eggs, separated	

1. If fish is cold-smoked, foil-bake at 180°C for 20-25 minutes.

2. Flake fish, removing skin and bones.

3. Melt butter in saucepan, blend in flour and cook 1-2 minutes until bubbling.

4. Gradually stir in milk and heat until boiling, add beaten egg yolks and fish.

5. Beat egg whites until stiff. Fold into hot fish mixture.

6. Pour into a lined and greased Swiss roll tin (25 cm x 30 cm).

7. Bake at 200°C for 12-15 minutes or until puffed and golden brown.

8. While this is cooking, make filling by combining all ingredients.

Light Meals

Open Crab Sandwiches

9. When fish mixture is cooked turn it onto a damp teatowel.

10. Carefully remove lining paper and spread with filling. Gently roll up roulade from the long side.

Serve hot or cold with a salad.

Light Meals

Fish-stuffed Baked Potatoes
Serves 4

1 x 220 g can fish, e.g. tuna, mackerel, drained and flaked
4 medium potatoes
2 Tbsp oil
30 g butter
½ cup milk or cream
1 Tbsp lemon juice
100 g cheese, chopped into 5-mm cubes
1 egg, beaten
salt and pepper to taste

1. Wash and dry potatoes. Brush skins with oil so they remain soft during cooking.
2. Bake at 200°C for 45-60 minutes, or until tender.
3. Cut potatoes in half and carefully scoop out flesh, leaving skins intact.
4. Mash half the potato (remaining potato is not required for this recipe). Add remaining ingredients and combine thoroughly.
5. Spoon filling into potato skins and bake at 180°C for 25 minutes.

Serve hot, unaccompanied or with a green salad.

Savoury Smoked Fish
Serves 4

400 g hot- or cold-smoked fish, skinned and boned
2 Tbsp butter
2 Tbsp flour
1 cup milk
75 g tomatoes, peeled and chopped
75 g tasty cheese, grated
1 Tbsp tomato sauce
salt and pepper to taste

1. Cut fish into 1.5-cm pieces.
2. Melt butter in a saucepan, blend in flour and cook 1-2 minutes until bubbling.
3. Gradually stir in milk and heat until boiling.
4. Add smoked fish to sauce. If fish has been cold-smoked, simmer 4-5 minutes, stirring constantly; otherwise, bring sauce to the boil.
5. Add tomatoes and heat through. Remove from heat.
6. Blend in grated cheese, tomato sauce and seasonings to taste.

Use as a filling for savouries or place in a greased ovenproof dish, sprinkle with parmesan cheese and breadcrumbs, brown under a preheated grill, and serve with a salad.

Light Meals

Savoury Bake

Serves 2

- 200 g hot- or cold-smoked fish, skinned and boned
- 1 tsp butter
- 1 onion, finely chopped
- 1 green pepper, finely chopped
- 1 firm tomato, chopped
- 1-2 pickled gherkins, sliced
- 1/3 cup mayonnaise (not salad dressing)
- 1/4 cup grated tasty cheese
- 1/2 cup crushed potato crisps or 1/4 cup bran flakes

1. Cut fish into 1.5-cm cubes.

2. Melt butter in a saucepan, add fish and onion and cook until onion is translucent. Remove from heat.

3. Combine chopped pepper, tomato, gherkins, mayonnaise and fish mixture.

4. Place in a lightly greased ovenproof dish and bake at 180°C for 15 minutes.

5. Sprinkle with grated cheese and crushed potato crisps or bran flakes.

6. Return to oven and cook a further 5 minutes until cheese has melted.

Serve with French bread or bread rolls.

Variation

1. Replace smoked fish with 200 g delicate- to medium-textured, skinless, boneless fish fillets.

MAIN COURSES

Camembert Surprise
Serves 4

- 4 large, medium- to firm- textured, skinless, boneless fish fillets
- 1 x 125 g packet camembert cheese
- ½ cup white wine
- ⅔ cup milk
- 2 Tbsp butter
- 1 Tbsp flour
- 1 tsp lemon juice
- 2 tsp chopped parsley

1. Cut camembert horizontally through centre to form 2 rounds. Cut each round in half.

2. Cut each fillet in half widthways. Place the tail end piece of the fillet, skinned side down, in an ovenproof dish.

3. Place a section of camembert on each piece of fish then top with remaining halves of the fish fillets, placed skinned side down.

4. Pour wine over the fish, cover and bake at 190°C for 15-20 minutes.

5. Drain cooking liquid off fish and add to milk to make up 1 cup of liquid. Keep fish hot while making sauce.

6. To make sauce: melt butter in a saucepan, add flour and cook 1 minute. Gradually stir in milk and cooking liquid and heat until sauce boils and thickens. Add lemon juice and parsley and cook a further minute.

Serve with crusty bread and a green salad.

Smoked Salmon and Caviar with Pasta
Serves 4

- 200-250 g smoked salmon cut into slivers (salmon offcuts are ideal)
- 2 Tbsp butter
- 1 Tbsp finely chopped shallot or onion
- 2 Tbsp flour
- 1 cup milk
- ¼ cup dry white wine
- salt and pepper to taste
- 2-3 Tbsp caviar

1. Melt butter in a saucepan, sauté shallot or onion until translucent.

2. Blend in flour and cook 1 minute until foaming.

3. Gradually stir in milk and heat until sauce boils.

Camembert Surprise

4. Add wine and cook 2-3 minutes.

5. Gently stir in salmon and cook a further 2 minutes. Check seasonings.

6. Just before serving, stir in 1 Tbsp caviar.

To serve, either blend the sauce into cooked pasta or pour over cooked pasta. Sprinkle with remaining caviar. Accompany with a green salad.

Main Courses

Foil-baked Fish

Whole fish, fish steaks and skinless, boneless fish fillets are suitable for foil-baking.

1. Cut pieces of foil large enough to wrap individual whole fish, steaks or fillets or include several in the same package.

2. Place fish on foil and add 1 or 2 of the following: a slice of lemon, orange, onion, tomato, green pepper, mushroom, celery, a sprig of parsley (including the stem where the most flavour is) or fresh dill, fennel, rosemary, basil or thyme. Season to taste with salt and pepper.

3. Bring edges of foil together at the top and fold over tightly to form a seal. Fold up each end of foil to seal and form a parcel.

4. Place on oven tray.

5. Bake at 200°C. Approximate times:

- Whole fish — fresh: for each 200 g allow 10 minutes
  frozen: for each 200 g allow 15 minutes
- Steaks or fillets — fresh: 10-15 minutes
  frozen: 20-30 minutes

Serve French style, 'en papillotte' — with the fish in foil on the dinner plate — or remove from foil before serving. Accompany with potatoes and vegetables or bread rolls and a salad.

Whole Fish with Tarragon

Serves 4

1 whole fish, approximately 1.5 kg, scaled and gutted
1 tsp cooking oil
2 tsp dried tarragon

Dressing
1 cup sour cream
1 Tbsp mild prepared mustard
2 tsp dried tarragon

1. Weigh fish to assist in calculating cooking time.

2. Lightly brush outside of fish with oil and sprinkle with tarragon.

3. Wrap fish in foil or place in a baking dish with cover. Bake at 200°C, allowing 10 minutes per 200 g if fresh or 15 minutes per 200 g if frozen.

4. To make dressing: combine all ingredients thoroughly. Chill.

Serve fish and sauce separately. Accompany with vegetables or a salad.

Foil-baked Fish

Wonderful Whisky-baked Fish

Serves 6-8

1 whole fish, about 700 g, scaled, gutted and eyes removed
2 Tbsp whisky
4-cm length of root ginger
1 carrot ring

1 olive stuffed with pimento (optional)
1 dsp soy sauce
1 dsp oil

1. Using a sharp knife, slash surface of fish in a criss-cross diamond pattern.

2. Place fish in an ovenware dish and pour whisky over.

3. Slice root ginger in matchstick-sized pieces and spread over fish.

4. Trim carrot ring to fit in eye socket of fish. Make a small hole in centre of carrot ring for half the olive, cut crosswise.

5. Cover dish and bake at 200°C for 15 minutes. Remove cover.

6. Mix together soy sauce and oil. Brush over partially cooked fish.

7. Return fish, uncovered, to oven and bake a further 15 minutes or until fish is cooked when tested.

Serve with potatoes and vegetables or crusty bread and a salad.

Mushroom Topping for Baked Fish

Serves 3-4

500 g skinless, boneless fish fillets
100 g mushrooms, finely chopped
½ cup grated cheese
salt and pepper to taste
¼ cup slivered almonds

1. Cut fillets into serving-sized pieces and place in a greased ovenware dish.
2. Combine mushrooms, cheese and seasonings.
3. Spread evenly over fillets. Sprinkle with slivered almonds.
4. Bake at 200°C for 15-20 minutes or until fish flakes when tested.

Serve with a salad and crusty bread.

Chinese-style Whole Fish

Serves 1

This dish is especially suitable for flounder and sole.

1 small, delicate- to medium-textured whole fish, up to 500 g, scaled and gutted
1 Tbsp finely chopped spring onion
1 dsp finely chopped root ginger
1 dsp soy sauce
¼ cup oil, heated

1. Foil-bake fish (see Foil-baked Fish on p. 92).
2. Combine spring onion and ginger. Place half this mixture on a heat-resistant shallow serving dish.
3. Place fish on the serving dish. Sprinkle over remaining spring onion and ginger, then soy sauce.
4. Slowly pour the very hot oil over fish.

Serve immediately with rice or bread and a green salad.

Baked Tartare Fish

Serves 3-4

500 g skinless, boneless fish fillets
¼ cup commercial or home-made tartare sauce (see Sauces)
¼ tsp curry powder
½ cup dry breadcrumbs

1. Cut fillets into serving-sized pieces.
2. Mix tartare sauce with curry powder and spread on 1 side of fish fillets.
3. Dip this first side into breadcrumbs, then repeat sauce and breadcrumb coating on other side.
4. Arrange in a single layer in a lightly greased baking dish.
5. Bake, uncovered, at 210°C for 10-15 minutes or until fish flakes when tested.

Garnish with lemon slices and serve with French-fried potatoes and a salad or vegetables.

Fish Baked with Leeks and Corn

Serves 4

500 g skinless, boneless fish fillets
2 Tbsp butter or oil
1 leek, finely sliced
1 x 310 g can whole kernel corn, drained or cream-style corn
½ cup grated cheese
¼ cup bran flakes or dried breadcrumbs
salt and pepper to taste

1. Cut fish into serving-sized pieces and place in a lightly greased baking dish.
2. Heat butter or oil in a frypan, add leek and sauté 5 minutes.
3. Cover fish with sautéed leek and drained corn or cream-style corn. Top with grated cheese and bran flakes or breadcrumbs. Season with salt and pepper.
4. Bake, uncovered, at 190°C for 15-20 minutes or until fish flakes when tested.

Serve with green vegetables and baked potatoes.

Main Courses

Fish in Caper Butter

Serves 3-4

500 g medium- to firm-textured, skinless, boneless fish fillets
60 g butter
1 Tbsp lemon juice
2 Tbsp capers, roughly chopped
2 Tbsp parsley, finely chopped

1. Cut fillets into serving-sized pieces.
2. Heat butter in a frypan until foaming.
3. Add fish and cook over a medium heat 3-6 minutes.
4. Add lemon juice, capers and parsley and cook a further 2-3 minutes until fish flesh turns white throughout.

Serve with sautéed potatoes and vegetables or a salad.

Fish with Lemon Butter

Serves 4

4 medium-textured fish fillets (skinless, boneless) or steaks
25 g butter, melted
2 Tbsp lemon juice

1. Place fish fillets or steaks in a greased ovenware dish.
2. Brush with melted butter and lemon juice.
3. Either bake at 180°C for 20-30 minutes; grill 10-15 cm from a preheated grill for 10-12 minutes, turning once; or cover with a paper towel and microwave on high, allowing 2-4 minutes for each 200 g.

Serve with potatoes and vegetables or crusty bread and a salad.

Creamy Tarragon Fillets

Serves 4

750 g skinless, boneless fish fillets
½ cup cream
1 Tbsp lemon juice
½ tsp sugar
½ tsp dried tarragon
1 Tbsp chopped parsley
salt and pepper to taste

1. Cut fish into serving-sized pieces and place in a greased ovenproof dish.
2. Combine cream, lemon juice, sugar, tarragon, parsley and seasonings. Pour over fish.
3. Bake at 190°C for 15-20 minutes or until the fish flakes when tested.

Serve with baked potatoes and a salad or vegetables.

Main Courses

Fish in Caper Butter

Simple Fish Curry

Serves 6

750 g medium- to firm-textured, skinless, boneless fish fillets
2 Tbsp butter
1 small onion, finely chopped
2 tsp curry powder
3 Tbsp flour
1 tsp sugar
1 tsp lemon juice
1 x 310 g can pineapple pieces and juice
¼ cup sultanas
salt and pepper to taste

1. Cut fish into 2-cm cubes.
2. Melt butter in a large saucepan, add onion and cook until translucent.
3. Blend in curry powder, flour, sugar and lemon juice. Cook until bubbling.
4. Gradually stir in pineapple pieces and juice. Cook until thickened.
5. Add cubed fish and sultanas. Simmer gently until fish is cooked, approximately 10 minutes, adding water if curry becomes too thick. Check seasonings.

Serve on a bed of rice.

Main Courses

Light and Spicy Fish Curry
Serves 4

500 g medium- to firm-textured, skinless, boneless fish fillets
3 Tbsp butter or oil
2 onions, finely chopped
1 tsp turmeric
1 tsp coriander
½ tsp chilli powder
½ cup coconut milk
1 cup unsweetened yoghurt
juice of 1 lemon
salt to taste

1. Cut fish into 2-cm cubes.
2. Heat oil or butter in a large saucepan, sauté onions until soft.
3. Add turmeric, coriander and chilli powder and cook 2 minutes.
4. Add cubed fish, coconut milk, yoghurt and lemon juice. Simmer gently, stirring occasionally, until fish is cooked — approximately 10 minutes. Season to taste with salt.

Serve on a bed of rice with a green salad.

Rolled Fish Fillets with Vegetables
Serves 4

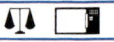

4 thin, medium-textured, skinless, boneless fish fillets (about 1 cm thick)
2 Tbsp butter
2 onions, finely chopped
1 clove garlic, crushed
1½ cups sliced mushrooms
1 x 425 g can tomatoes, drained and chopped
2 Tbsp lemon juice
½ tsp sugar
¼ tsp dried basil
salt and pepper to taste

1. Roll up fish fillets lengthwise, starting with the narrow end. Secure with toothpicks if necessary. Place in a baking dish.
2. Melt butter in a saucepan, add onions and garlic and cook until translucent.
3. Add mushrooms and cook 3-4 minutes.
4. Add tomatoes, lemon juice, sugar and basil. Cook 2-3 minutes then remove from heat. Check seasonings. Pour over fish.
5. Cover and bake at 190°C for 15-20 minutes or until the fish flakes when tested.

Serve with a green salad and rice or potatoes.

Main Courses

Fish Fillets Provencale

Serves 3-4

500 g skinless, boneless fish fillets
2 tomatoes, skinned and chopped
3 olives, de-stoned and chopped
2 spring onions, finely chopped
pinch sugar
salt and pepper to taste

1. Cut fish into serving-sized pieces and place in an ovenproof dish.

2. Combine tomatoes, olives, spring onions, sugar, salt and pepper and spread over fish.

3. Cover with a lid or foil and bake at 180°C for 20 minutes or until fish flakes when tested.

Serve with baked potatoes and green vegetables.

Fish Mornay

Serves 4

500 g medium- to firm-textured, skinless, boneless fish fillets
3 Tbsp butter
3 Tbsp flour
1½ cups milk
1 bay leaf
½ cup grated cheese
1 Tbsp lemon juice
salt and pepper to taste
¼ cup grated cheese, extra
¼ cup dried breadcrumbs or bran flakes

1. Cut fish into 2-cm cubes.

2. Melt butter in a saucepan.

3. Blend in flour and cook 1-2 minutes until foaming.

4. Gradually stir in milk and bay leaf and heat until sauce boils. Remove from heat.

5. Remove bay leaf and discard. Add cubed fish, cheese, lemon juice and seasonings.

6. Pour into a greased ovenware dish. Sprinkle with extra cheese and breadcrumbs or bran flakes.

7. Bake at 190°C for 15-20 minutes or until fish is cooked and topping is brown.

Serve with baked potatoes and vegetables or a salad.

Variation

1. In step 2 add ½ cup chopped bacon and sauté bacon until cooked. In step 5 add ½ cup cooked asparagus pieces or green beans.

Jenny's Crunchy Creation

Fried Whole Fish

Serves 4

8 small whole fish, scaled and gutted e.g. garfish, creamfish
flour for coating
salt and pepper to taste
1 egg, beaten
dried breadcrumbs for coating
2 Tbsp butter
1 Tbsp lemon juice
1 Tbsp chopped parsley

1. Season flour with salt and pepper and coat fish with this mixture.
2. Dip floured fish in beaten egg.
3. Coat with breadcrumbs and place on a rack in refrigerator for at least 10 minutes to allow crumbs to set.
4. Melt butter in a frypan, add lemon juice and parsley.
5. Fry fish gently, turning once until golden brown and cooked through, approximately 3 minutes each side.

Serve with French-fried potatoes and a salad.

Main Courses

Jenny's Crunchy Creation
Serves 4

750 g medium-textured, skinless, boneless fish fillets
flour for coating
salt and pepper to taste
100 g butter, melted
breadcrumbs for coating

1. Cut fish into serving-sized pieces.
2. Season flour with salt and pepper. Coat fillets with this mixture.
3. Dip fillets in melted butter.
4. Coat with breadcrumbs.
5. If time permits, stand coated fish on a rack in refrigerator for at least 10 minutes to set the breadcrumbs.
6. Lay fillets on a greased tray and place 10-15 cm from a preheated grill. When crumbs are golden brown, turn fish carefully and cook other side, until fish flakes when tested with a fork.

Serve immediately with sautéed potatoes and a salad.

Variations

1. *Garlic.* Crush 1-2 cloves and add to butter before melting.
2. *Herbs.* Add 1 tsp dried or 1 Tbsp chopped fresh herbs to breadcrumbs.
3. *Citrus.* Replace breadcrumbs with 150 g chopped nuts and grated rind of 1 orange, mixed together.

Creamy Fish
Serves 3-4

500 g skinless, boneless fish fillets
1 cup cream, whipped
½ cup grated cheese
salt and pepper to taste

1. Cut fish into serving-sized pieces and arrange in a lightly greased baking dish.
2. Spread whipped cream over fish and sprinkle with grated cheese and seasonings.
3. Bake, uncovered, at 190°C for 20 minutes or until fish flakes when tested.

Serve with baked potatoes and a salad or vegetables.

Variation

1. *Creamy Caper Fish.* In step 2, sprinkle 1 Tbsp chopped capers over cream-covered fish before sprinkling with grated cheese.

Main Courses

Fish Cakes
Serves 3-4

500 g delicate- to medium-textured, skinless fish fillets
1 onion, finely chopped
1-2 sticks celery, finely chopped
2 eggs
1 cup cooked mashed potato
½ cup grated tasty cheese (optional)
salt and pepper to taste
½ cup dried breadcrumbs
oil for baking or frying

1. Foil-bake, steam, poach or microwave fish fillets until white throughout. Flake, removing bones.

2. Combine flaked fish, onion, celery, eggs, potato, cheese if desired, and seasonings.

3. Shape mixture into cakes or patties and coat with dried breadcrumbs.

4. Bake, uncovered, in a lightly oiled ovenware dish at 200°C for 25 minutes or shallow fry in hot oil for 3-4 minutes on each side. Drain on absorbent paper.

Serve with a salad.

Variations

1. *Smoked Fish Cakes.* Replace fish with 500 g delicate- to medium-textured hot- or cold-smoked fish. If cold-smoked, foil-bake at 180°C for 25-30 minutes. Flake fish, removing skin and bones and add in step 2.

Seafood Fritters
Makes about 24 fritters

250-300 g seafood (delicate- to medium-textured skinless, boneless fish fillets and shellfish e.g. mussels, pipis, tuatuas)
2 cups flour
2 tsp baking powder
¼ tsp baking soda
1 tsp salt
2 eggs
½-1 cup milk
¼ tsp dried basil
1 tsp grated lemon rind
1 Tbsp lemon juice
pepper to taste
3 Tbsp finely chopped onion
oil and/or butter for shallow frying

1. Finely chop fish and mince shellfish.
2. Combine flour, baking powder, baking soda and salt in a large bowl.
3. Beat eggs and half the milk together, then stir into dry ingredients.
4. Add fish and shellfish, basil, lemon rind and juice, pepper and onion.
5. Add more milk if necessary to form a mixture that can be dropped off spoon to form flat fritters about 2-3 cm thick.
6. Heat oil and/or butter in a frypan.
7. Shallow fry fritters 4 minutes first side, 3 minutes second side. Drain on absorbent paper.

Serve hot or cold with a salad and French-fried potatoes.

Smoked Fish Pilaf

Serves 4

300 g delicate- to medium-textured, hot- or cold-smoked fish
1 packet tomato soup
3¼ cups water
1 onion, finely chopped
1 green pepper, deseeded and finely chopped
2 tomatoes, skinned and chopped roughly
1¼ cups long grain rice

1. If fish is cold-smoked, foil-bake at 180°C for 20-25 minutes.
2. Flake fish, removing skin and bones.
3. In a casserole or heavy-based frypan, mix tomato soup to a paste with some of the water. Add remaining water.
4. Add fish, onion, green pepper, tomatoes and rice.
5. Cook casserole at 180°C for 1 hour or cook in a frypan for 15-20 minutes.

Serve with a tossed salad.

Variation

1. Canned smoked fish may be used.

Main Courses

Seafood Lasagne

Serves 4-5

400 g medium- to firm-textured, skinless, boneless fish fillets
250 g pasta e.g. lasagne, macaroni spirals
2 Tbsp butter
1 clove garlic, crushed
1 onion, finely chopped
½ cup finely chopped celery
1 carrot, grated
3 Tbsp tomato paste
1 tsp dried basil
2 tsp lemon juice
1 tsp sugar
1 cup chopped spinach or silver beet
salt and pepper to taste

Cheese Sauce
2 Tbsp butter
2 Tbsp flour
1 bay leaf
300 ml milk
2 Tbsp lemon juice
¾ cup grated cheese
salt and pepper to taste
¼ cup grated cheese, extra

1. Cook pasta in a large saucepan of boiling water until tender. Drain and rinse under cold water.

2. Melt butter in a saucepan, add garlic, onion, celery and carrot. Cook until vegetables are soft.

3. Add tomato paste, basil, lemon juice and sugar and mix thoroughly.

4. Cut fish into 2-cm cubes and add to tomato mixture. Cook gently until fish is just cooked.

5. Stir spinach into fish and allow to heat through. Season to taste then remove from heat.

6. To make Cheese Sauce: melt butter in a saucepan, add flour and cook 1-2 minutes. Gradually blend in milk and bay leaf until the sauce boils and thickens. Remove from heat. Add lemon juice and cheese to the sauce. Check seasonings.

7. Stir the pasta into the cheese sauce.

8. Spread half the pasta sauce over base of a greased shallow ovenproof dish, then cover with the tomato fish mixture. Top with remaining pasta sauce and sprinkle with extra cheese.

9. Bake at 180°C for 20 minutes or until heated through and golden brown. Serve with a green salad.

Marinara

Serves 4

500 g seafood (medium- to firm-textured, skinless, boneless fish fillets and shellfish e.g. oysters, scallops, mussels)
2 Tbsp oil
1 onion, finely chopped
¼ tsp dried basil
½ tsp paprika
¼ tsp dried oregano
2 Tbsp white wine (optional)
1 x 425 g can tomatoes and juice
salt and pepper to taste

1. Cut fish into 2-cm cubes. Steam open shellfish and remove shellfish meat from shells. Discard shells that do not open.
2. Heat oil in a frypan, add onion and sauté until soft.
3. Add basil, paprika and oregano and cook 2-3 minutes.
4. Add wine, if desired, and tomatoes and juice. Simmer until thick and pulpy, approximately 5-10 minutes.
5. Add cubed fish and shellfish and cook gently until fish turns white throughout. Check seasonings.

Serve immediately over pasta.

Marinara

Lemon Ginger Fish
Serves 4

500 g medium- to firm-textured, skinless, boneless fish fillets

Marinade

½ cup lemon juice
1 cup chicken stock or water
1 Tbsp sherry
2 tsp grated root ginger

¼ tsp salt
3 Tbsp sugar or honey
2 Tbsp cornflour

1. Cut fish into serving-sized pieces.
2. Mix all marinade ingredients together.
3. Marinate fish in marinade in refrigerator for at least 1 hour.
4. Drain fish and reserve marinade.
5. Place fish 10-15 cm from a preheated grill and cook 2-3 minutes each side.
6. Place marinade in a saucepan and bring slowly to the boil, stirring constantly.

To serve, place fish on a bed of rice and pour sauce over. Accompany with a salad or vegetables.

Spicy Cold Fish
Serves 6-8

1 medium to large fish, scaled and gutted e.g. snapper, tarakihi, trevally
cold water
¼ cup lemon juice
1 onion, sliced

Marinade

1 cup vinegar
½ cup water
2 bay leaves
½ tsp basil
½ tsp garam masala

1. Place fish in a large frypan or ovenproof dish and just cover with cold water.
2. Add lemon juice and onion. Cover and place either on top of stove or in oven at 180°C. Poach fish gently for approximately 30 minutes or until flesh flakes when tested with a fork. Drain fish.
3. Combine all marinade ingredients and pour over fish.
4. Place in refrigerator and marinate overnight. Drain and remove bay leaves.

Garnish with sprigs of parsley and serve with rice and a salad.

Main Courses

Soused Fish

Any type of medium- to firm-textured fish may be soused. These recipes are ideal for whole fish, skinless boneless fillets, steaks or fish such as sardines and pilchards.

Spicy Soused Fish

Serves 2

6 sardines or pilchards or
  1 small whole fish or 2 fish
  fillets or steaks

<u>Sousing Liquid</u>
½ cup cider vinegar
½ cup water
½ tsp salt
black pepper
2 Tbsp brown sugar
2 bay leaves
¼ tsp cinnamon
¼ tsp thyme
¼ tsp chilli powder
1 onion, sliced
celery leaves
parsley stalks

1. If using whole fish, scale and gut fish and cut off head and tail. Put fish in an ovenware dish and add other ingredients. Cover and bake at 180°C, allowing 15 minutes for every 500 g of fish. Remove from oven and, leaving fish in liquid, cool and chill at least overnight but preferably 2 days.

2. If using fish fillets or steaks, place fish in an ovenware dish. Bring remaining ingredients to the boil, then pour over fish. Cover and bake at 180°C for 10-15 minutes. Remove from oven, cool and chill as above for whole fish.

To serve, remove fish from liquid and garnish with parsley and slices of lemon, tomato or cucumber. Accompany with a green salad and crusty bread.

Vegetable Soused Fish
Serves 2

6 sardines or pilchards or
1 small whole fish or 2 fish
fillets or steaks

Sousing Liquid

½ cup cider vinegar
½ cup white vinegar
¼ cup water
4 black peppercorns
2 bay leaves

1 carrot, sliced
1 onion, sliced
2 parsley stalks
celery leaves (optional)

1. If using whole fish, scale and gut fish and cut off head and tail.
2. Place all ingredients, except fish, in a saucepan and reduce by rapid boiling to half quantity. Cool to lukewarm.
3. Place fish in a pan, strain stock over fish and bring slowly to the boil.
4. Allow to simmer gently for 1 minute. Remove pan from heat and cool.
5. Cover dish and keep in refrigerator until required (keeps 3-4 days).

To serve, drain off liquid and place fish on a lettuce-lined plate. Accompany with a salad and fresh bread.

Crumb-topped Fillets
Serves 4

750 g skinless, boneless fish fillets
3 Tbsp butter
1 clove garlic, crushed (optional)
¾ cup fresh breadcrumbs
½ tsp grated lemon rind
½ cup grated tasty cheese (optional)
salt and pepper to taste

1. Cut fish into serving-sized pieces; arrange in a lightly greased baking dish.
2. Melt butter in a saucepan and if desired, add garlic and cook 1 minute.
3. Add breadcrumbs and stir to coat with butter. Cook 3-5 minutes until golden. Remove from heat.
4. Add lemon rind and if desired, combine with cheese. Season to taste with salt and pepper.
5. Sprinkle crumbs over fish.
6. Bake at 190°C for 15-20 minutes or until fish flakes when tested.

Serve with a salad or vegetables.

Paella

Serves 8

- 500 g medium- to firm-textured, skinless, boneless fish fillets
- 12 mussels, tuatuas or pipis
- 150 g cooked prawns (optional)
- ½ cup white wine
- ½ cup water
- ¼ cup oil
- 200 g chicken fillets, cut in strips
- 2 onions, chopped
- 2 cloves garlic, crushed
- 1 green pepper, deseeded and cut into strips
- 1 red pepper, deseeded and cut into strips
- 4 cups long grain rice
- 1 x 440 g can tomatoes and juice
- ¼ tsp powdered saffron or turmeric
- 2 Tbsp chicken stock powder
- 5 cups water
- salt and pepper to taste

1. Cut fish into 2-cm cubes.

2. Wash shellfish. Remove beards, if present. Place shellfish in saucepan with wine and water. Cover and heat until shellfish open 1-2 cm. Drain shellfish and reserve liquid. Remove shellfish meats from 8 shellfish and cut into quarters. (Leave 4 in shells for garnishing.)

3. Heat oil in a large, heavy-based frypan, add fish and fry quickly on all sides until just cooked. Remove from pan and drain on absorbent paper.

4. Add chicken and fry until golden brown. Remove from pan and drain.

5. Add onions, garlic, green and red peppers and rice to frypan and cook for 3 minutes or until rice is transparent.

6. Measure reserved shellfish cooking liquid and add sufficient water to make up 2 cups liquid. Add to the frypan with the tomatoes and juice, saffron or turmeric, chicken stock powder and water.

7. Mix thoroughly and heat until boiling. Lower heat, cover and simmer gently for 10 minutes or until liquid is absorbed and rice is tender.

8. Stir in cooked fish, chopped shellfish and chicken and allow to heat through 1-2 minutes. Season to taste with salt and pepper.

Serve on a large platter garnished with the 4 shellfish still in their shells.

Main Courses

Fisherman's Pie

Serves 4-6

300 g delicate- to medium textured, hot- or cold-smoked fish, skinned and boned
3 Tbsp butter
1 onion, finely chopped
3 Tbsp flour
1½ cups milk
250 g mixed vegetables, fresh (finely diced), canned or frozen
salt and pepper to taste
Topping: see suggestions below

1. Cut fish into 1.5-cm cubes.
2. Melt butter in a saucepan, add onion and cook until translucent.
3. Blend in flour and cook 1 minute until foaming.
4. Gradually stir in milk and heat until the sauce comes to the boil. Add cubed fish and vegetables.
5. Simmer 2-3 minutes, season to taste.
6. Place in a greased ovenware dish. Use 1 of the toppings suggested below.
7. Bake at 150°C for 30 minutes.

Toppings

1. *Diced fresh bread.* Remove crusts and cut into 5-mm cubes. Sprinkle over pie.
2. *Buttered breadcrumbs.* Melt 2 Tbsp butter and combine with ¾ cup dried breadcrumbs and, if desired, ½ cup grated cheese. Sprinkle over pie.
3. *Potato crisps and cheese.* Combine ½ cup crushed potato crisps and ½ cup grated cheese. Sprinkle over pie.
4. *Mashed potato.* Spread or pipe 2 cups cooked mashed potato over pie. Top with grated cheese if desired.

Variations

1. In step 4, add 2 chopped hard-boiled eggs when adding the vegetables.
2. Replace smoked fish with 300 g delicate- to medium-textured, skinless, boneless fish fillets.
3. This dish may also be cooked in a pastry shell. Roll out 300 g flaky or short pastry into 2 circles. Use 1 circle to line the base and sides of a 20-cm pie dish, add fish filling. Moisten top edge of pastry in pie dish. Cover pie with second circle of pastry. Crimp edges together and cut slits in top layer of pastry to allow steam to escape. Bake at 200°C for 15 minutes then 150°C for a further 15 minutes.

Main Courses

Fisherman's Pie

Savoury Fish Casserole

Serves 6

750 g skinless, boneless fish fillets
3 Tbsp oil
4 tomatoes, peeled and chopped
2 onions, chopped
1 clove garlic, crushed
1 red or green pepper, deseeded and chopped
1 stalk celery, sliced
3 rashers bacon, chopped
1 Tbsp brown sugar
1 tsp paprika
¼ cup white wine
salt and pepper to taste

1. Cut fish fillets into serving-sized pieces and place in a casserole dish.
2. Heat oil in a frypan and add tomatoes, onions, garlic, pepper, celery, bacon, brown sugar and paprika. Simmer until thick and pulpy.
3. Add wine and cook 2 minutes. Season to taste with salt and pepper.
4. Pour tomato mixture over fish. Cover with a lid or foil.
5. Bake at 180°C for 30 minutes or until fish flakes when tested.

Sprinkle with chopped parsley and serve with French bread.

Main Courses

Traditional Oyster and Veal Pie

Serves 4-6

- 12 oysters and juice
- 500 g flaky pastry
- 1 Tbsp oil
- 500 g thick flank or topside veal, cut into 1-cm cubes
- 1 Tbsp cornflour
- 1 onion, sliced
- 1 carrot, sliced
- salt and pepper to taste

1. Roll out flaky pastry. Cut a large circle to line base and sides of a 20-cm pie dish, and a smaller circle for the pie top. Line pie dish and set aside pie top.
2. Heat oil in a frypan, add veal and cook until brown, approximately 2-3 minutes. Remove veal from pan and drain on absorbent paper.
3. Measure oyster juice and add sufficient water to make up ½ cup of liquid. Combine with cornflour and add to brownings in frypan. Cook until thickened, stirring constantly.
4. Combine oysters, veal, sauce, vegetables and seasonings and place in pastry-lined pie dish.
5. Moisten top edge of pastry in pie dish. Cover with pie top. Crimp edges together and cut slits in pie top to allow steam to escape.
6. Bake at 190°C for 30-40 minutes or until pastry is golden.

Serve with a green salad and tomatoes or vegetables.

Pisces Pasta Dish

Serves 6

- 1 x 425 g can fish cutlets or smoked fish, undrained
- 1 cup macaroni
- 3 Tbsp butter
- 1 onion, finely chopped
- 1 Tbsp curry powder
- 2 Tbsp flour
- 1 x 425 g can tomatoes, chopped with juice
- salt and pepper to taste

1. Cook macaroni in boiling salted water until tender. Drain and rinse.
2. Melt butter in a saucepan, sauté onion until translucent.
3. Add curry powder and flour and cook 1 minute.
4. Gradually add chopped tomatoes and juice. Cook 3 minutes.
5. Add cooked macaroni and undrained fish cutlets or smoked fish, heat through. Season to taste with salt and pepper.

Garnish with chopped parsley and serve with a green salad.

Paua Steaks

Serves 4

4 paua
2 Tbsp butter
1 large onion, cut in thick rings
salt and pepper to taste

1. To prepare paua: remove gut and cut off foot and thick outer edge on foot side. If the pharynx (red-coloured, located in the area of the mouth) is still attached, it is best removed. To tenderise paua either beat with the flat surface of a meat tenderiser or the bottom of a milk bottle or marinate with a crushed, raw ripe kiwifruit for 1 to 2 hours.

2. Melt butter in a heavy-based frypan, add onion rings and stir to coat with butter. Season lightly with salt and pepper.

3. Place paua on top of onion rings. Cook for 6 minutes on 1 side, turn and cook a further 4 minutes. Take care not to burn onion rings.

Serve immediately with vegetables.

Devilled Paua

Serves 4

2 paua
¼ cup oil
1 Tbsp chopped onion
1 Tbsp chopped green pepper
1 clove garlic, crushed
½ cup dry white wine
¼ cup tomato sauce
1 tomato, skinned and chopped
pinch cayenne pepper or ¼ tsp dry mustard
4 tsp cornflour
2 Tbsp water
salt to taste

1. Prepare and tenderise paua, as in step 1 of Paua Steaks (above), then thinly slice.

2. Heat oil in a saucepan and sauté onion, pepper and garlic.

3. Add paua, wine, tomato sauce, chopped tomato and cayenne pepper or mustard. Simmer 2-3 minutes.

4. Stir in cornflour and water mixed to a smooth paste. Simmer until thickened. Season to taste with salt.

Serve with crusty bread and a green salad or vegetables.

Main Courses

Spiced Crab
Serves 3-4

250 g crab meat
1 Tbsp butter
2 Tbsp oil
2 onions, finely chopped
½ tsp coriander

½ tsp turmeric
½ cup coconut milk
2 Tbsp unsweetened yoghurt
salt to taste

1. Heat butter and oil in a saucepan, add onions and cook gently for 5 minutes until golden.

2. Add coriander and turmeric and cook on high heat for 1 minute, stirring constantly.

3. Lower heat and add crab meat. Cook 3-5 minutes.

4. Add coconut milk, yoghurt and salt to taste. Cook a further 2 minutes until thick and creamy.

Serve with fresh bread and a salad or with rice.

Mussels in Wine
Serves 3

18 large or 24 small mussels
1½ cups dry white wine
4 spring onions, finely chopped
1 clove garlic, crushed
½ tsp dried thyme

50 g butter, softened
2 Tbsp flour
black pepper to taste
¼ cup cream
2 Tbsp finely chopped parsley

1. Scrub and rinse mussels and remove beards. In a large saucepan place mussels, white wine, spring onions, garlic and thyme. Cover and bring to the boil.

2. Simmer gently for 4-6 minutes or until mussels open 1-2 cm. Drain, reserving liquid. Cover mussels to keep warm.

3. In a small saucepan, boil reserved liquid, uncovered, until reduced to half quantity.

4. Cream together softened butter and flour and whisk into the liquid. Stir until smooth and thick. Season to taste with pepper.

5. Add cream and parsley. Heat through, but do not boil.

Arrange warm mussels in serving bowls and spoon sauce over. Accompany with fresh crusty bread and a green salad.

Main Courses

Mussels and Squid in Basil Sauce
Serves 4

12 fresh mussels or mussel meats
1 cleaned squid tube
1 Tbsp butter
1 clove garlic, crushed
2 tomatoes, peeled and chopped
¼ cup dry white wine
1 Tbsp tomato paste
¼ cup cream
2 Tbsp chopped fresh basil or
 ½ tsp dried basil
½ tsp sugar
salt and pepper to taste

1. If using fresh mussels follow directions for cleaning and cooking (see p. 36). Remove meat from shells.

2. Roughly chop 9 mussel meats.

3. Cut squid tube into thin rings. Put squid rings into a saucepan of boiling water. When water comes to the boil and squid turns opaque, drain and cool under cold running water.

4. Heat butter in a saucepan. Add garlic, tomatoes, wine and tomato paste and simmer 10 minutes. Purée in food processor or blender with 3 reserved mussel meats and cream.

5. Return to pan and simmer 5 minutes.

6. Stir in roughly chopped mussels, squid rings, basil and sugar. Reheat but do not boil. Check seasonings.

Serve over pasta and accompany with a green salad.

Matsuo Squid
Serves 4-6

2 cleaned squid tubes (about
 500 g in total), cut into strips,
 1 cm x 3 cm
2 Tbsp oil
1 onion, finely chopped
½ cup dry white wine
2 Tbsp tomato paste
1-2 Tbsp finely chopped parsley
3 cups cooked long grain rice
salt and pepper to taste

1. Heat oil in a frypan, add onion and cook 3-5 minutes.

2. Add wine, tomato paste and parsley and cook 5 minutes.

3. Add cooked rice and cook on high, stirring occasionally, until very hot.

4. Finally add prepared squid and cook only until squid turns white, approximately 2-3 minutes. Season to taste.

Serve immediately with a tossed salad.

Main Courses

Baked Stuffed Squid

Serves 8 as an appetiser or 4-6 as a main course

2 cleaned squid tubes (about 500 g in total)
Stuffing
2 Tbsp oil
1 clove garlic, crushed
1 stick celery, finely chopped
¼ cup tomato purée
1 egg, beaten

1 cup cooked long grain rice
1 x 150 g can shrimps, drained
2 Tbsp lemon juice
salt and pepper to taste
Sauce
¼ cup tomato purée
¼ cup water
1 Tbsp oil

1. To make stuffing: heat oil in a saucepan, sauté garlic and celery 2-3 minutes. Remove from heat and combine with tomato purée, beaten egg, rice, shrimps, lemon juice and seasonings to taste.

2. Stuff cleaned squid tubes with stuffing and secure ends with toothpicks.

3. Mix sauce ingredients together in a small baking dish.

4. Place stuffed squid tubes in dish and spoon sauce over.

5. Cover and bake at 180°C for 30 minutes.

To serve, remove toothpicks and slice into 1-cm rings. Accompany with salad.

Squid with Black Bean Sauce

Serves 4-6

2 cleaned squid tubes (about 500 g in total), cut into strips, 1 cm x 3 cm
2 Tbsp oil
1-2 cloves garlic, crushed
2 tsp grated root ginger

4 spring onions, chopped
2 Tbsp black bean sauce*
2 Tbsp dry sherry
1 tsp sugar
2 Tbsp soy sauce

1. Heat oil in a frypan, sauté garlic and ginger for 2 minutes.

2. Add spring onions and cook a further 2 minutes.

3. Combine black bean sauce, sherry, sugar and soy sauce and add to pan. Cook 2 minutes.

4. Add prepared squid and cook on high for 15-30 seconds or until squid turns opaque and starts to curl.

Serve immediately over rice.

*Black bean sauce may be purchased from delicatessens or oriental food merchants.

Main Courses

Creamy Mussel Sauce for Pasta

Serves 4 as an entrée or 2 as a main course

24 fresh mussels or mussel meats
50 g butter
1 onion, finely chopped
1 clove garlic, crushed
½ cup white wine
250 g sour cream
2 Tbsp tomato paste
salt and pepper to taste

1. If using fresh mussels, follow directions for cleaning and cooking (see p. 36). Remove meat from shells. Chop mussel meats finely or mince.

2. Melt butter in a saucepan, sauté onion and garlic until onion is translucent.

3. Add wine and simmer until liquid is reduced to half quantity.

4. Stir in sour cream, tomato paste and chopped or minced mussels. Heat sauce but do not boil. Season to taste with salt and pepper.

Serve over hot cooked pasta and sprinkle with finely chopped parsley and/or grated parmesan cheese. Accompany with a green salad.

Breadcrumb Coating for Fish and Shellfish

Serves 3-4

750 g medium- to firm-textured, skinless, boneless fish fillets or 24 shellfish
½ cup flour
1 egg
¼ tsp salt
pepper to taste
1 tsp oil
¾ cup dried breadcrumbs
oil for frying

1. Coat fish or shellfish in flour.

2. Beat egg with a fork and add salt, pepper and oil. Dip each fillet of fish or shellfish into egg.

3. Coat fish or shellfish with breadcrumbs then place crumbed seafood on a rack in refrigerator for at least 10 minutes. This allows crumbs to set and prevents coating from falling off during cooking.

4. Shallow or deep fry 2-3 minutes in hot oil until golden brown and cooked through.

5. Drain and keep hot until ready to serve.

Serve with lemon wedges, French-fried potatoes and a salad.

Main Courses

Batter for Seafood

Sufficient to coat 500 g seafood

½ cup flour	pepper to taste
¾ cup water	1 egg white, beaten
3 Tbsp oil	flour for coating
¼ tsp salt	oil for frying

1. Mix flour to a paste by gradually adding water.

2. Combine with oil, salt and pepper.

3. Fold in beaten egg white. Thin with more water to a pouring consistency if necessary.

4. To use: coat seafood pieces in extra flour then dip in batter. Shallow or deep fry in hot oil at approximately 180-190°C until golden brown and cooked through.

Tempura Batter for Seafood

Sufficient to coat 500 g seafood

½ cup flour	pepper to taste
¾ cup ice water	1 egg white, beaten
3 Tbsp cooking oil	flour for coating
¼ tsp salt	oil for frying

1. Mix flour to a paste by gradually adding water.

2. Blend in oil, salt and pepper.

3. Fold in beaten egg white. Thin with more water to a pouring consistency if necessary.

4. To use: coat seafood in extra flour then dip in batter. Shallow or deep fry in hot oil at approximately 180-190°C until golden brown and cooked through.

Batter for Seafood

Beer Batter for Seafood

Sufficient to coat 450 g seafood

1 cup flour
salt and pepper to taste
pinch sugar

1 cup beer, freshly opened or flat
flour for coating
oil for frying

1. In a bowl combine all dry ingredients.
2. Gradually blend in beer to make a smooth paste of the desired consistency.
3. To use: coat seafood in extra flour then dip in batter. Shallow or deep fry in hot oil at approximately 180-190°C until batter is crisp and golden and seafood is cooked.

SALADS

Seafood, Feta Cheese and Pasta Salad

Serves 5-6

- 375 g seafood (medium-textured, skinless, boneless fish fillets, and shellfish e.g. mussels, pipis, scallops)
- 300 g spiral pasta or macaroni
- 200 g feta cheese, cut into cubes or 1 cup grated tasty cheese
- ½ cup chopped spring onions
- ½ cup chopped hazelnuts
- 1 red pepper, sliced into thin strips

Yoghurt Garlic Dressing
- ¾ cup natural yoghurt
- ½ cup mayonnaise
- 2 Tbsp lemon juice
- 1 clove garlic, crushed
- salt and pepper to taste

1. Foil-bake, steam or microwave fish until it flakes when tested with a fork. Cut into 1.5-cm cubes. Steam open shellfish and remove meat from shells. Discard shellfish which do not open. Cool all cooked seafood.
2. Cook pasta in boiling salted water until just tender. Drain, rinse and cool.
3. In a bowl, place cooked seafood and pasta, cubed or grated cheese, spring onions, hazelnuts and red pepper.
4. To make Yoghurt Garlic Dressing: combine yoghurt, mayonnaise, lemon juice and garlic. Season to taste.
5. Pour dressing over salad ingredients and mix gently.
6. Chill for at least 1 hour before serving.

Serve in a salad bowl lined with lettuce leaves.

Crunchy Mussel Salad

Serves 6 as an entrée or 3 as a main course

- 18 marinated or smoked mussels
- 4 sticks celery, finely chopped
- 2 spring onions, finely chopped
- 1 red apple, cored and chopped
- 2 Tbsp mayonnaise or salad dressing

1. Combine marinated or smoked mussels, celery, spring onions, apple and mayonnaise or salad dressing.
2. If time permits, chill before serving.

Serve with crusty French bread.

Salads

Curry Salmon Salad

Serves 4

250 g cooked and flaked salmon (salmon offcuts are ideal)
200 g raw macaroni or pasta shells
75 g sunflower seeds
1 spring onion, sliced
1 cup sliced celery
2 cups frozen peas, thawed

Curry Dressing
1 cup mayonnaise
1 Tbsp curry powder
1 Tbsp prepared mustard
2 Tbsp lemon juice
1 clove garlic, crushed
salt to taste

1. Cook macaroni or pasta in boiling salted water until tender. Drain, rinse and cool.
2. Combine macaroni, sunflower seeds, spring onion, celery and peas.
3. To make Curry Dressing: combine mayonnaise, curry powder, mustard, lemon juice and garlic. Add salt to taste.
4. Combine curry dressing and macaroni mixture. Chill.
5. Before serving, add salmon to macaroni and toss lightly.

Serve garnished with parsley and lemon wedges.

Variation

1. Replace macaroni with 1 cup long grain rice.

Apricot Favourite

Serves 3-4

500 g medium-textured, skinless, boneless fish fillets
1 x 450 g can apricots, drained
1 cup sliced celery
salt to taste

Dressing
¼ cup mayonnaise
¼ cup sour cream
2 Tbsp lemon juice
2 spring onions, finely chopped

1. Foil-bake, steam or microwave fish until it flakes when tested with a fork. Allow fish to cool then cut into 1.5-cm cubes.
2. Combine fish, apricots, celery and salt.
3. To make dressing: mix together mayonnaise, sour cream, lemon juice and spring onions.
4. Add dressing to fish and stir gently. Chill.

Serve in lettuce cups.

Salads

Smoked Fish and Pasta Salad

Smoked Fish and Pasta Salad
Serves 3-4

- 250 g hot- or cold-smoked fish, skinned and boned
- 2 cups pasta shells
- 2 Tbsp oil
- 1 onion, finely chopped
- 1 cup raw or cooked assorted vegetables, chopped e.g. celery, peppers, carrots, beans

Seafood Dressing
- ½ cup mayonnaise
- 1 Tbsp tomato sauce
- 2 Tbsp lemon juice
- salt and pepper to taste

1. If fish is cold-smoked, foil-bake at 180°C for 20-25 minutes.
2. Cut fish into 1.5-cm pieces.
3. Cook pasta in boiling salted water until just tender (do not overcook). Drain, rinse and cool.
4. Heat oil in frypan. Sauté onion until translucent. Add smoked fish pieces and heat through.
5. Place cooked pasta in a mixing bowl, add smoked fish mixture and prepared vegetables.
6. To make Seafood Dressing: combine mayonnaise, tomato sauce and lemon juice. Season to taste.

7. Gently mix seafood dressing into smoked fish mixture. Chill at least 1 hour before serving.

Serve with crusty French bread.

Smoked Fish Salad

Serves 4

750 g hot- or cold-smoked fish, skinned and boned
1 x 310 g can sliced beetroot, drained
¼ cup sliced gherkins
1 cup chopped cucumber

Dressing
1 cup sour cream
1 Tbsp finely chopped parsley
1 spring onion, finely chopped
salt and pepper to taste

1. If fish is cold-smoked, foil-bake at 180°C for 25-30 minutes.
2. Cut smoked fish into 2-cm cubes.
3. Chop beetroot and mix with gherkins, cucumber and smoked fish.
4. To make dressing: mix together sour cream, parsley, spring onion, salt and pepper until smooth.
5. Gently combine dressing and smoked fish mixture.
6. Chill until ready to serve.

Serve on a bed of lettuce leaves.

Refreshing Tuna Salad

Serves 4

1 x 310 g can tuna, drained and flaked
2 cucumbers, peeled and thinly sliced
1 onion, finely chopped
1½ cups cooked long grain rice

Dressing
1 cup sour cream
2 Tbsp lemon juice
1 Tbsp finely chopped parsley
salt and pepper to taste

1. Place tuna, cucumber, onion and rice in a bowl.
2. To make dressing: mix together sour cream, lemon juice and parsley. Season to taste.
3. Pour dressing over salad ingredients and toss lightly to coat.
4. Chill at least 1 hour before serving.

Serve in salad bowl lined with lettuce leaves.

Salads

Tropical Squid Salad

Serves 4

500 g squid rings	1 cup drained canned unsweetened pineapple pieces
Dressing	
½ cup mayonnaise	1 Tbsp chopped parsley
¼ cup sour cream	¼ tsp paprika
1 Tbsp chilli sauce	3-4 drops tabasco
1 spring onion, finely chopped	salt and pepper to taste

1. Place squid rings in a saucepan of boiling water. When water comes to the boil and squid turns white, drain immediately and cool under cold running water.

2. To make dressing: combine mayonnaise, sour cream, chilli sauce, spring onion, parsley, paprika, tabasco, salt and pepper.

3. Add pineapple and squid to dressing. Chill for at least 30 minutes before serving.

Serve on a bed of lettuce leaves.

Mussel and Chive Salad

Serves 4

24 mussels	1 cup water
2 onions, sliced	½ cup lemon juice or white wine
6 parsley stalks	
Dressing	
¼ cup oil	1 clove garlic, crushed
¼ cup dry white wine	1 spring onion, finely chopped
½ cup lemon juice	½ tsp sugar
¼ tsp finely chopped root ginger	salt and pepper to taste

1. Scrub and rinse mussels. Remove beards.

2. Place onions, parsley stalks, water and lemon juice or white wine in a large saucepan and bring to the boil.

3. Add mussels, cover and allow mussels to steam until shells open 1-2 cm. Cool. Discard mussels that do not open.

4. To make dressing: place oil, white wine, lemon juice, root ginger, garlic, spring onion and sugar in a screw-top jar. Shake well and season to taste.

5. Spoon dressing over cooled mussels. Chill for 30 minutes before serving.

Serve garnished with lemon wedges.

Mighty Mussel Salad

Serves 4

1 x 375 g pottle marinated mussels, drained
½ small lettuce
60 g button mushrooms
½ green pepper
1 stalk celery
8 cm length of cucumber, peeled
2 small zucchini
1 small avocado
2 hard-boiled eggs, sliced

Dressing
1 Tbsp wine vinegar
1 tsp prepared mustard
1 tsp castor sugar
1 Tbsp mayonnaise
2 Tbsp finely chopped parsley
1 Tbsp oil
1 Tbsp water
salt and pepper to taste

1. Cut each mussel into 4 pieces.
2. Separate lettuce leaves and wash well in cold water. Drain and tear into pieces.
3. Wash and slice mushrooms, green pepper, celery and cucumber thinly.
4. Peel zucchini and cut into strips.
5. Peel avocado and cut into cubes.
6. Combine mussels and prepared vegetables in a large bowl.
7. Arrange sliced eggs on the bottom of a salad plate or bowl.
8. To make dressing: in a small bowl, beat together vinegar, mustard, castor sugar, mayonnaise and parsley. Gradually beat in oil and water. Season to taste.
9. Pour dressing over salad and toss well to coat. Pile salad onto salad plate or bowl. Chill.

Salads

Marinated Fish

Serves 6 as an entrée or 3-4 as a main course

500 g medium- to firm-textured, skinless, boneless fish fillets, cut into 1-cm cubes

1 small onion, cut into large chunks

1½ cups lemon juice or ½ cup lemon juice and 1 cup white vinegar

1. Combine the fish, onion, lemon juice and vinegar in a plastic bag or a non-aluminium container.

2. Cover and refrigerate for 6-8 hours or until the fish becomes white throughout.

3. Drain fish and discard marinade. Remove onion chunks.

4. If desired mix the fish with a seafood dressing (see Sauces) or use marinated fish in any of the recipes which follow.

Garnish with slices of lemon, tomato, cucumber or chopped spring onions.

Marinated Fish

Summer Vegetable Marinated Fish

Serves 6 as an entrée or 3-4 as a main course

500 g marinated cubed fish
½ cup chopped cucumber
½ cup grated carrot
½ cup sliced celery
1 green pepper, finely chopped

2 spring onions, sliced
2 Tbsp yoghurt or sour cream
2 Tbsp mayonnaise
dash of tabasco
salt and pepper to taste

1. Combine all ingredients thoroughly. Check seasonings.
2. Chill for 30 minutes before serving.

Serve in lettuce cups.

Marinated Fish Salad with Yoghurt Dressing

Serves 6 as an entrée or 3-4 as a main course

500 g marinated cubed fish
1 cup unsweetened yoghurt
1 cup sliced celery

dash tabasco sauce
¼ tsp sugar
salt and pepper to taste

1. Combine all ingredients thoroughly. Check seasonings.
2. Chill for 30 minutes before serving.

Serve sprinkled with paprika.

Kokada Salad

Serves 6 as an entrée or 3-4 as a main course

500 g marinated cubed fish
200 ml canned coconut cream or milk
2 Tbsp chopped chives or spring onions

1 red pepper, finely chopped
salt to taste
freshly ground black pepper

1. Mix all ingredients together.
2. Chill at least 30 minutes before serving.

Serve with a fresh green salad or in lettuce cups.

Salads

Fish and Vegetable Platter

Fish and Vegetable Platter

Serves 4

750 g medium-textured, skinless, boneless fish fillets	100 g green beans, cut lengthwise and lightly blanched
2 Tbsp lemon juice	½ cup French dressing
8 large lettuce leaves	**Parsley Dressing**
2 tomatoes, cut into wedges	¼ cup chopped parsley
½ cucumber, sliced	2 Tbsp capers
100 g mushrooms, cut in half	2 Tbsp white vinegar
2 medium carrots, peeled and cut into thin strips	1 Tbsp chopped chives
	1 cup mayonnaise

1. To make Parsley Dressing: combine parsley, capers, vinegar and chives in a food processor and process until smooth. Fold parsley mixture into the mayonnaise and mix well. Cover and chill 1 hour.

2. Brush fish fillets with lemon juice. Foil-bake, steam or microwave fillets until they just flake when tested with a fork. Allow fish to cool a little, then cut into 1.5-cm cubes.

3. Line a large serving platter with lettuce leaves.

4. Coat fish with parsley dressing and pile into the centre of the platter.

5. Toss the individual lots of prepared vegetables in French dressing and arrange in groups around the fish.

6. Chill until ready to serve.

Serve with French bread.

Marinated Squid

Serves 10-12 as a pre-dinner snack, 6 as a main course

2 cleaned squid tubes (about 500 g in total)	½ cup oil
½ cup lemon juice	1 clove garlic, crushed
	2-3 Tbsp chopped parsley

1. Cut squid tubes into thin strips or small pieces. Put squid in a saucepan of boiling water. When water comes to the boil and squid turns white, drain immediately and cool under cold running water.

2. Combine lemon juice, oil, garlic, parsley and prepared squid in a non-aluminium container.

3. Refrigerate for 4-24 hours.

Drain and serve either as a pre-dinner snack or for lunch with a green salad and bread.

BARBECUES

Barbecuing Tips

1. Before filling the barbecue with charcoal, line it with foil. This reflects the heat and saves cleaning afterwards. The charcoal can be wrapped and reused if any remains, or alternatively the ashes can be wrapped and discarded.

2. Before lighting the barbecue, grease barbecue rack well with butter or oil to prevent fish sticking to it.

3. The traditional method of cooking fish on the barbecue is to gut and scale the fish then wrap it in damp newspaper. Place the fish parcel either on the hot coals or on a rack above them. The cooking time depends on the size of the fish and the heat of the fire. Don't allow the newspaper to burn through.

4. A long-handled, hinged wire grill to hold the fish securely is ideal to prevent the fish flaking as cooking nears completion.

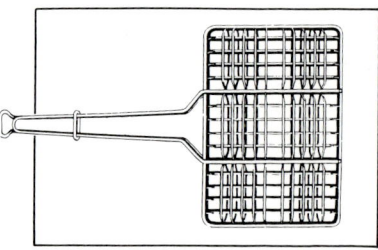

5. Special wire fish baskets are available and are ideal for large whole fish.

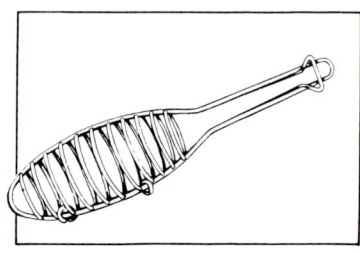

6. For an economical whole fish barbecue holder, buy some chicken wire, wash thoroughly in hot soapy water and wrap around whole fish before barbecuing. This holds fish firmly together (turn with tongs or use an oven mitt).

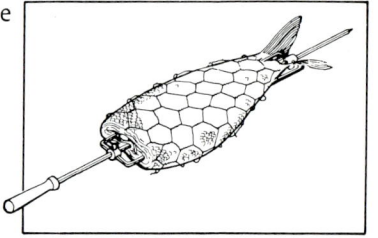

7. Remember that even whole fish take much less time to cook than steaks or chicken pieces. If you are having a mixed grill, put these other meats on to cook much earlier (along with baked potatoes, corn cobs, etc.).

8. To allow easier heat penetration and therefore quicker cooking, leave gaps between the items threaded onto skewers and also the foods on the barbecue.

9. Use tongs instead of forks so that the flesh isn't punctured and the juices don't escape.

10. Keep a pump-spray bottle of water handy. Use it to spray on flare-ups but don't soak the coals.

11. Soak the grill rack in hot soapy water while you eat. If it won't fit in the sink, place the rack on well-soaked newspaper and cover with more wet newspaper. Burned-on food usually steams loose and allows the grill to be easily washed later.

12. Have a waste bin handy for scraps.

13. Have plenty of paper napkins or kitchen paper to wipe hands on.

14. To save washing metal skewers, purchase packets of bamboo skewers from hardware or kitchen shops. Soak in cold water before use to prevent charring.

Barbecued Whole Fish

Serves 6

medium-textured whole fish e.g. snapper, tarakihi, trevally, mullet (about 2 kg)
1 large onion, cut into rings
1 lemon, cut into slices

sprigs of either fresh rosemary, fennel or marjoram
melted butter or oil
salt and pepper to taste

1. Clean, gut and scale fish and cut off fins. Leave head and tail on.

2. Slash fish on both sides at 5-cm intervals. Insert rings of onion, slices of lemon and sprigs of herbs alternately.

3. Brush with melted butter or oil, sprinkle with seasonings and place in a fish basket or wrap in foil.

4. Barbecue over a moderate heat for 15 minutes on each side (total of 30 minutes) or until fish flakes.

Serve with a salad and baked potatoes.

Variation

1. *Barbecued Stuffed Whole Fish.* Use 1 of the following stuffings to fill cleaned gut cavity of whole fish. (Omit onion, lemon and herbs from step 2 if desired.)

Apricot and Celery Stuffing

Makes 2½ cups

60 g butter
1 large onion, finely chopped
1 cup sliced celery
½ cup chopped dried apricots
²⁄₃ cup chopped walnuts
½ cup fresh white breadcrumbs
1 Tbsp chopped parsley
salt and freshly ground pepper to taste
grated rind and juice of ½ lemon

1. Melt butter in a saucepan, add onion and celery and cook until tender.
2. Add apricots and walnuts and cook a further 2 minutes.
3. Mix in breadcrumbs, parsley, salt, pepper, lemon rind and juice.
4. Use to stuff gut cavity of a whole fish.

Variation

1. *Apricot and Almond Stuffing.* Omit celery and walnuts and add ¼ cup raisins and ¼ cup chopped blanched almonds in step 2. Makes 1½ cups.

Tomato and Mushroom Stuffing

Makes 1½ cups

30 g butter or margarine, melted
2 large tomatoes, peeled and chopped
125 g mushrooms, sliced
1 Tbsp chopped parsley
salt and pepper to taste

1. Melt butter in a saucepan then add tomatoes, mushrooms and parsley.
2. Cook gently 3-4 minutes. Add salt and pepper to taste.
3. Allow to cool until warm before stuffing the gut cavity of a whole fish.

Hazelnut-Prune Stuffing

Makes 1½ cups

1 Tbsp butter or margarine
1 onion, chopped
½ cup roughly chopped hazelnuts or brazil nuts
2 rashers bacon, chopped
1 chicken stock cube
1 Tbsp boiling water
¾ cup prunes, stones removed
grated rind of 2 lemons
1 cup cooked brown rice
salt and pepper to taste

1. Melt butter or margarine in a large frypan. Add onion and fry until soft, about 5 minutes.

2. Add hazelnuts or brazil nuts and bacon and fry until bacon is crisp.

3. Add stock cube and boiling water to onion mixture and simmer for 2 minutes.

4. Remove from heat and add prunes, lemon rind and rice. Mix together well, adding salt and pepper to taste.

5. Use to stuff cavity of a whole fish.

Top to bottom: Apricot and Celery, Hazelnut-Prune, Tomato and Mushroom Stuffing

Barbecues

Tarragon and Paprika Stuffing

Makes 1¼ cups

- 2 Tbsp butter
- 1 Tbsp finely chopped onion
- 2 Tbsp finely chopped celery
- 2 Tbsp grated apple
- 2 rashers bacon, chopped
- 1 cup fresh breadcrumbs
- ¼ tsp dried tarragon
- ¼ tsp salt
- grind black pepper
- 2 Tbsp lemon juice
- ½ tsp paprika

1. Melt butter in a saucepan, then add onion, celery, apple and bacon. Cook 3-4 minutes until onion is soft.

2. Mix in breadcrumbs, tarragon, salt, pepper, lemon juice and paprika.

3. Use to stuff gut cavity of a whole fish.

Celery and Apple Stuffing

Makes 2 cups

- 1 cup chopped celery
- 2 apples, peeled and grated
- 1 onion, finely chopped
- 1 Tbsp raisins
- 1 tsp sugar
- salt and pepper to taste

1. Place celery, grated apples, onion, raisins and sugar in a small bowl and mix well until combined.

2. Season to taste with salt and pepper.

3. Use to stuff gut cavity of a whole fish.

Rice and Raisin Stuffing

Makes 2 cups

- 1 large onion, finely chopped
- ½ cup raisins
- 1 cup cooked rice
- ¼ cup chopped almonds
- ½ cup chopped parsley
- 30 g butter or margarine, melted
- salt and freshly ground pepper to taste
- 1 egg, beaten

1. In a bowl mix together onion, raisins, rice, almonds, chopped parsley and melted butter or margarine.

2. Season to taste with salt and pepper and bind together with beaten egg.

3. Use to stuff gut cavity of a whole fish.

Rice and Vegetable Stuffing

Makes 2½ cups

25 g butter	1½ cups cooked long grain rice
1 stalk celery, finely chopped	1 Tbsp chopped parsley
½ green pepper, finely chopped	¼ tsp salt
100 g mushrooms, finely chopped (optional)	grind black pepper
	1 Tbsp lemon juice
1 small onion, finely chopped	

1. Melt butter in a saucepan and sauté chopped celery, green pepper, mushrooms and onion until tender but not brown.

2. Mix sautéed vegetables and any remaining butter from the pan with cooked rice, parsley, salt, pepper and lemon juice.

3. Use to fill gut cavity of a whole fish.

Caper and Cream Cheese Stuffing

Makes 1 cup

250 g cream cheese	2 Tbsp lemon juice
1 Tbsp capers	salt and pepper to taste

1. Combine cream cheese, capers, lemon juice and seasonings. Mix well.

2. Fill cleaned gut cavity of whole fish with prepared stuffing.

Marinated Whole Fish for the Barbecue

Medium- to firm-textured fish are suitable for marinating, which adds flavour, and then barbecuing. For each kg of fish, use the following quantities.

½ cup olive oil	sprig parsley with stem
½ cup lemon juice	½ tsp salt
1 bay leaf	grind black pepper
sprig thyme	

1. Mix marinade ingredients together. Place fish in a non-aluminium container or plastic bag. Pour marinade over. Leave at least 1 hour.

2. Remove fish from marinade and grill or barbecue until fish is cooked on both sides (to prevent it falling to pieces, turn only once). Brush frequently with marinade.

Serve with a salad or fresh vegetables and baked potatoes.

Barbecues

Fish Kebabs

Oyster Kebabs

Makes 4 x 20-cm skewers

18 oysters, drained
¼ cup lemon juice
¼ cup chopped parsley
1 red pepper

18 thin slices of Veronese salami or krakauer
4 saté sticks or fine kebab skewers

1. Combine lemon juice and parsley in a small shallow dish.

2. Deseed pepper and cut into chunks.

3. Dip a slice of salami or krakauer in the lemon juice/parsley combination.

4. Place an oyster on the coated surface of the salami, fold salami around oyster, then thread onto saté stick or skewer, piercing both oyster and salami. Add a piece of pepper, then another salami-wrapped oyster, and so on, until skewer is full.

5. Place 12 cm from hot coals and cook for 4-6 minutes, turning once during cooking. Alternatively, they may be cooked under a preheated grill for the same time.

Serve with a tossed green salad or unaccompanied as an entrée.

Fish Kebabs

Makes about 20 x 20-cm skewers

- 750 g medium- to firm-textured, skinless, boneless fish fillets, cut into 2.5-cm cubes
- ½ cup vegetable oil
- 3 Tbsp vinegar
- ½ tsp salt
- grind black pepper
- 2 Tbsp finely chopped onion or 2 tsp fresh rosemary or oregano
- 100 g fresh small tomatoes, quartered
- 1 green pepper, deseeded and cut into 2.5-cm squares
- 3 rashers thick bacon, cut into 2.5-cm squares
- 150 g button mushrooms or large mushrooms cut into 2.5-cm squares
- 3 bananas, peeled and sliced into 2.5-cm lengths
- 20 x 20-cm skewers

1. Place oil, vinegar, salt, pepper and onion or herbs in a screw-top jar. Shake well.
2. Place cut-up fish, tomatoes, green pepper, bacon, and mushrooms into a large bowl. Pour marinade over. Toss to coat. Place in refrigerator for at least 1 hour. Toss occasionally.
3. Drain off marinade and reserve it to baste kebabs while grilling. Thread fish onto skewers with marinated ingredients and sliced bananas.
4. Cook under a preheated grill or on a barbecue approximately 10 minutes, turning occasionally. Baste with marinade during cooking.

Serve on a bed of rice or with baked potatoes.

Roasted Shellfish

1. If shellfish have been gathered from the sand, leave in a bucket of salt water in a cool place for 24 hours to allow sand to be filtered from them.
2. Scrub shells thoroughly.
3. Place shellfish on grill 10 cm from the hot coals. Roast until the shells open 1-2 cm.
4. Serve with plain or garlic butter or tartare sauce.

Ideal for shellfish such as pipis, tuatuas, oysters etc.

Butterflied Sole or Flounder

Allow 1 whole gutted sole or flounder per person.

1. Scale the sole (flounder has no scales). Cut off side fins but leave head and tail on.

2. Place fish on a chopping board, belly side down. Working from head towards tail, with a sharp knife cut through skin on left side just inside fins on the outer edge from head to tail. Lift up skin and flesh and with knife blade held flat, ease flesh from the bones right to the edge of the backbone.

3. Repeat on right side.

4. Turn sole over and repeat filleting on underside. This will give 4 'fillets' attached only along backbone.

5. With kitchen scissors, cut bones along edge of the backbone, i.e. remove both sides of the skeleton leaving the central backbone to hold the flesh together.

6. Stuff both sides with stuffing and foil-bake on barbecue for 15 minutes, or barbecue on rack 4 minutes on each side.

Seafood Stuffing

Makes ¼ cup

1 Tbsp butter	grind black pepper
1 Tbsp chopped onion	squeeze lemon juice
4 oysters, chopped or 2 Tbsp shrimps	¼ tsp grated lemon rind (optional)
¼ tsp salt	

1. Melt butter and sauté chopped onion until translucent.

2. Mix in remaining ingredients.

3. Use to stuff the pockets of a prepared sole or flounder, or double the recipe for a larger fish.

SAUCES

Mayonnaise

Makes 1 cup

1 egg	2 Tbsp lemon juice
½ tsp salt	200 ml salad oil
½ tsp dry mustard	

1. Place egg, salt, mustard, lemon juice and 50 ml oil in blender or food processor. Blend slowly to combine.

2. Gradually add the remaining 150 ml oil in a slow stream, blending all the time.

Use as a basis for other sauces such as Pink Mayonnaise and Tartare Sauce.

N.B. Mayonnaise contains egg and is often used as a thickening agent in cooked recipes. In such recipes salad dressing, which has no egg, must not be used.

Herb Mayonnaise

Makes 1 cup

1 cup mayonnaise	1 tsp dried tarragon
1 Tbsp finely chopped parsley	½ tsp dried chervil
1 tsp lemon juice	salt and pepper to taste
1 Tbsp finely chopped chives	

1. Mix together mayonnaise, parsley, lemon juice, chives, tarragon and chervil until well combined.

2. Season to taste with salt and pepper. Chill.

Suitable to serve with fish cooked by any method.

Pink Mayonnaise

Makes ½ cup

½ cup mayonnaise
1 Tbsp tomato paste
1 clove garlic, crushed
salt and pepper to taste

1. Mix together mayonnaise, tomato paste and crushed garlic until well combined.
2. Season to taste with salt and pepper. Chill.

Suitable to serve with fish cooked by any method.

Tartare Sauce

Makes 1¼ cups

1 cup home-made or commercial mayonnaise
1 Tbsp finely chopped capers
1 Tbsp finely chopped gherkin
2 Tbsp finely chopped parsley (optional)
1 Tbsp finely chopped onion (optional)

1. Combine all ingredients together.

Suitable to serve with fish cooked by any method.

Cocktail Sauce (Thousand Island Dressing)

Makes 1½ cups

1 cup cream, whipped
¼ cup tomato purée or sauce
¼ cup mayonnaise or salad dressing
½ tsp vinegar or lemon juice
1 tsp Worcestershire sauce or ¼ tsp tabasco sauce

1. Fold all ingredients into the whipped cream.

Serve over marinated fish, squid, or shellfish.

Barbecue Sauce

Makes 1 cup

½ cup water
½ cup tomato sauce
1 Tbsp Worcestershire sauce
1 Tbsp vinegar
1 Tbsp brown sugar
1 Tbsp cornflour
¼ tsp salt
grind black pepper

1. Mix all ingredients together and heat through, stirring constantly, until boiling.

Serve hot with fried, grilled or foil-baked fish.

Fresh Tomato Sauce

Makes ½ cup

2 Tbsp oil
1 clove garlic, crushed
4-5 tomatoes, peeled and chopped
½ tsp dried sweet basil
½ tsp dried thyme
¼ tsp black pepper
pinch sugar
salt to taste

1. Heat oil. Cook garlic, tomatoes and seasonings gently for 5 minutes.

Serve over hot fish.

Garlic Butter

25 g butter
1 clove garlic, crushed

1. Cream butter and garlic together.

Serve over hot fish.

Variations

1. *Herb Butter.* Replace garlic with 1 Tbsp finely chopped capers, 1 Tbsp finely chopped parsley and 1 Tbsp finely chopped chives.
2. *Savoury Butter.* Replace garlic with ¼ stalk celery, chopped finely, and 2 Tbsp finely chopped onion.

Sauces

Vinaigrette Sauce
Makes 1 cup

½ cup olive oil
½ cup lemon juice
2 cloves garlic, crushed
1 tsp dried oregano
1 Tbsp chopped fresh basil
1 Tbsp chopped parsley
salt and pepper to taste

1. Mix together oil, lemon juice, garlic, oregano, basil and parsley.
2. Season to taste with salt and pepper. Chill.

Serve with grilled or foil-baked fish.

Spiced Yoghurt Sauce
Makes 1 cup

1 cup natural yoghurt
¼ cup sour cream
1 Tbsp apricot jam
1 Tbsp peach chutney
2 tsp tomato sauce
1 tsp curry powder
1 tsp turmeric
salt and pepper to taste

1. Combine yoghurt, sour cream, jam, chutney, tomato sauce, curry powder and turmeric, using a whisk or beater.
2. Season to taste with salt and pepper. Chill.

This delicious sauce may be served with fish cooked by any method.

Creamy Cucumber Sauce
Makes 1½ cups

1 cup sour cream
¾ cup peeled, seeded and finely chopped cucumber
2 Tbsp mayonnaise
1 Tbsp vinegar
½ tsp salt

1. Combine all ingredients thoroughly.
2. Cover and chill at least 1 hour to blend flavours.

Serve with hot or cold seafood.

Clockwise from top left: Vinaigrette Sauce, Creamy Cucumber Sauce, Spiced Yoghurt Sauce, Pink Mayonnaise

Sweet and Sour Sauce

Makes 2 cups

2 Tbsp cooking oil
1 onion, sliced in rings
1 clove garlic, crushed
1 tsp grated root ginger
½ cup sliced carrot
½ cup sliced celery or green or red pepper

½ cup water
¼ cup vinegar
2 tsp soy sauce
1 Tbsp brown sugar
2 tsp cornflour
cold water to mix

1. Heat oil in saucepan and cook onion, garlic and ginger 1 minute.
2. Add carrot and celery or pepper and cook 1 minute.
3. Add water, vinegar, soy sauce, brown sugar and heat until simmering.
4. Blend in cornflour and water mixed to a smooth paste. Stir until sauce boils and thickens to the desired consistency.

Serve over battered fried fish or poached fish.

Economical Hollandaise Sauce
Makes 1 cup

2 Tbsp butter	1 cup milk
2 Tbsp flour	2 egg yolks
¼ tsp salt	2 Tbsp butter (extra)
shake pepper	2 dsp lemon juice

1. Melt butter in saucepan. Add flour, salt and pepper and cook 1-2 minutes until bubbling.

2. Gradually blend in milk and stir until sauce boils.

3. Beat egg yolks together and add a little of the hot sauce to them. Then add this egg mixture back into the sauce. (This helps prevent lumps forming.) Cook gently for 2 minutes. **N.B.** Do not boil sauce after adding egg yolks.

4. Add the extra butter. Stir until melted. Add lemon juice.

Serve hot over baked, poached or steamed fish.

Variations

1. *Cheese or Mornay Sauce.* Make sauce as above using first 5 ingredients and steps 1 and 2. Add ¼ cup grated cheese to the cooked sauce. Do not boil after cheese has been added.

2. *Parsley Sauce.* Make sauce as above using first 5 ingredients and steps 1 and 2. Add 2 Tbsp chopped parsley to the cooked sauce.

Tangy Herb Sauce
Makes 1 cup

1 Tbsp finely chopped fresh mixed herbs (use fresh thyme, chervil, chives, parsley or basil)	½ tsp lemon juice
	freshly ground black pepper
	1 Tbsp Dijon mustard
1 cup natural yoghurt	salt and pepper to taste

1. Combine herbs, yoghurt, lemon juice and black pepper.

2. Add mustard and beat well. Chill.

3. Before serving, season to taste.

Serve with baked, steamed or microwaved fish.

Onion and Parsley Sauce

Makes about 1½ cups

3 Tbsp butter
1 cup thinly sliced onions
2 dsp flour
1 cup milk
¼ cup finely chopped parsley
1½ tsp lemon juice
salt and pepper to taste

1. Melt butter in a saucepan, add onions and cook over a low heat until tender, approximately 15 minutes.
2. Blend in flour and cook 1-2 minutes until bubbling.
3. Gradually stir in milk and heat until sauce boils. Simmer 1 minute.
4. Add parsley and lemon juice and season to taste with salt and pepper.

Serve hot over steamed, poached, foil-baked or microwaved fish.

Blue Cheese Sauce

Makes 1½ cups

⅓ cup sour cream
100 g blue vein cheese, crumbled
¼ cup mayonnaise
⅓ cup milk
1 tsp prepared English mustard
2 tsp lemon juice
2 Tbsp finely chopped spring onions
salt and pepper to taste

1. Place sour cream, blue vein cheese, mayonnaise, milk, mustard and lemon juice in a food processor or blender and process until smooth.
2. Stir in spring onions and season to taste with salt and pepper.
3. If a food processor or blender is not available, push the blue vein cheese through a sieve and combine thoroughly with other ingredients.

Serve with poached or grilled fish.

Piri Piri Sauce

Makes ¾ cup

¾ cup mayonnaise
¼ tsp cayenne pepper
1 Tbsp tomato paste or sauce
1 dsp brandy (optional)

1. Combine all ingredients together.
2. Keep in a screw-top jar in refrigerator.

Serve with squid and crumbed seafood.

GARNISHES

A simple garnish can transform a meal. As well as adding an extra touch of colour and interest it transmits the message that the cook really cares.

Garnishes are far more simple to create than they appear. The aim should be to make them 'good enough to eat'. Therefore, components should be edible foods so this can in fact happen.

The use of garnishes such as lemon flowers means the juice can be used on the seafood as well as providing an attractive accompaniment. Parsley need not be the only fresh herb you use — select any fresh herbs suited to fish to add colour and even a subtle perfume to your finished dish, such as rosemary, fennel, dill or celery leaves.

Carrot Twists

1. Cut a 6-cm section from a peeled carrot.

2. Cut section lengthwise into slices, approximately 3 mm thick.

3. Make a 1-2 cm slit lengthwise in the centre of each slice.

4. Soak slices in a salt solution (1 Tbsp salt dissolved in 1 litre water) for at least 10 minutes. Rinse.

5. When pieces are very soft, push one corner of carrot slice through slit in centre, and pull it through slit to form a twisted rectangle.

Apple Feathers

1. Cut an unpeeled apple into 6 equal-sized wedges.

2. Place first apple wedge skin-side up. Slice through skin towards core on each side but don't cut right through. Slice until the 2 cuts meet to form a large V-shaped slice.

3. Remove the larger V of apple and set aside. Repeat above process on the smaller remaining V of apple 3 times more until there are 4 V-shaped slices.

4. Reassemble wedges, but spread them slightly to show both flesh and skin.

5. Coat with lemon juice to stop browning.

6. Repeat steps 2 to 5 with the 5 remaining apple wedges.

Garnishes

Clockwise from top left: Lemon Loops, Apple Feather, Courgette Palm, Carrot Twists, Flying Fish, Spring Onion Brush

Spring Onion Brush

1. Cut roots off spring onion leaving as much white base as possible.

2. Slice green part of spring onion lengthwise into many thin slivers. Do not cut into the white base.

3. Place the sliced spring onion into a bowl of ice cold water and leave 10-15 minutes until slivers curl up.

Lemon Loops

1. Cut lemons in half from top to bottom, i.e. through the stem.
2. To obtain semi-circular lemon slices, thinly slice each lemon half from skin to stem.
3. Starting on one side of each lemon slice, carefully make a cut through the pith between skin and flesh, and work around semi-circle until approximately 1 cm of skin remains attached to the lemon.
4. Curl and tuck the cut piece of skin under.

Flying Fish

1. Slice cucumber lengthwise at approximately $1/3$ of cucumber width.
2. Place this narrow strip flat-side down on a board and slice off one end diagonally at about a 30-degree angle.
3. Keeping the piece flat-side down, make a series of diagonal slices, parallel to the cut diagonal edge, about 3 mm apart. Cut only $3/4$ of the way through so a spine holds slices together. The more slices made the further the final fish bends.
4. Soak sliced cucumber in a salt solution (1 Tbsp salt dissolved in 1 litre water) for at least 10 minutes. Rinse.
5. Starting at the diagonally cut end fold each alternating slice towards the uncut cucumber end then under so a small loop is formed. Repeat for 5 or 6 alternating slices.

Lemon Twists

1. Slice lemons thinly and remove pips.
2. Lay slices on a board and slit from centre point to edge on 1 side only.
3. Hold slice between fingers and twist 1 cut side forward and 1 back to form a lemon twist.
4. Add sprigs of parsley if desired.

Use for garnishes on seafood cocktails or any fish dish.

Courgette Palm

1. Cut a 10-cm section from an unpeeled courgette.
2. Cut section in half lengthwise.
3. Place flat side down on a board. Cut away the 2 sides, leaving a flat piece about 2 cm wide and 10 cm long.
4. With skin-side upwards cut notches across the width to reveal the white flesh. Cut notches at 5-mm intervals leaving 15-20 cm at one end for the 'trunk'.
5. Cut five 7-cm slits lengthwise through the notched length to form leaves.
6. Soak in a salt solution (1 Tbsp salt dissolved in 1 litre water) for 10 minutes. Rinse.
7. Spread leaves to form a palm.

Tomato or Lemon Flowers

1. Cut whole lemon or tomato in a zigzag pattern around centre with a sharp pointed knife (a small vegetable knife is ideal). Push knife to centre core with each cut. Separate the two halves.
2. Cut slice off base to enable it to sit flat.
3. Place sprig of parsley or stuffed olive in centre of cut 'flowers' if desired.

These are especially suitable for serving with simply cooked fish dishes where a squeeze of lemon is desired.

INDEX

A

Apple Feathers 146
Apricot
    and Celery Stuffing 132
    Favourite 121
Asparagus
    Fish and Asparagus Flan 84
    Fish and Asparagus Soup 61

B

Baked
    Fish Baked with Leeks and Corn 95
    Mushroom Topping for Baked Fish 94
    Stuffed Squid 116
    Tartare Fish 95
    Wonderful Whisky-baked Fish 93
Barbecue Sauce 141
Barbecued Stuffed Whole Fish 131
Barbecued Whole Fish 131
Barbecuing Tips 130
Batter
    Beer Batter for Seafood 119
    for Seafood 118
    Tempura Batter for Seafood 118
Blue Cheese Sauce 145
Bouillabaisse-style Soup 61
Breadcrumb Coating for Fish and Shellfish 117
Butterflied Sole or Flounder 138

C

Camembert Surprise 90
Caper and Cream Cheese Stuffing 135
Carrot Twists 146
Celery
    and Apple Stuffing 134
    Apricot and Celery Stuffing 132
    Fish and Celery Flan 84
Cheese or Mornay Sauce 144
Chinese-style Whole Fish 94
Cocktail Sauce (Thousand Island Dressing) 140
Country Chowder 65
Courgette Palm 149
Crab
    How to Remove Crab Meat 40
    Open Crab Sandwiches 86
    Pâté 51
    Pawpaw and Crab Entrée 71
    Spiced 114
Cream-baked Scallops 75
Creamy Caper Fish 101
Creamy Cucumber Sauce 142
Creamy Fish 101
Creamy Mussel Sauce for Pasta 117
Creamy Tarragon Fillets 96
Creamy Seafood Soup 67
Crepes
    Oyster and Spinach 73
    Stacked Seafood 72
    Standard Crepe Recipe 72
Crispy Seafood Surprises 55
Crumb-topped Fillets 108
Crumbed Squid Rings 70
Crunchy Fish Won Tons 57
Crunchy Mussel Salad 120
Curry
    Dressing 121
    Light and Spicy Fish Curry 98
    Salmon Salad 121
    Simple Fish Curry 97

D, E

Devilled Paua 113
Economical Hollandaise Sauce 144

F

Fish
    and Asparagus Flan 84
    and Asparagus Soup 61
    and Celery Flan 84
    and Leek Flan 84
    and Spinach Flan 84
    and Vegetable Platter 129
    Baked with Leeks and Corn 95
    Cakes 102
    Chowder 64
    Creamy 101
    Creamy Caper 101
    Fillets Provencale 99
    Fish-Cheese Puff 82
    Fish-stuffed Baked Potatoes 88
    Foil-baked 92
    Fried Whole 100
    in Caper Butter 96
    Kebabs 137
    Mornay 99
    Pâté 51
    Soufflé 84
    with Lemon Butter 96
Fisharettes 54
Fisherman's Pie 110
Fluffy Oyster Balls 53
Flying Fish (garnish) 148
Foil-baked Fish 92
Fresh Tomato Sauce 141

G, H

Garlic Butter 141
Grilled Scallop Kebabs 73
Hazelnut-Prune Stuffing 132
Herb Butter 141
Herb Marinated Mussels 76
Herb Mayonnaise 139

I, J, K

Jenny's Crunchy Creation 101
Jiffy Mussel Chowder 63
Jo's Spanish Soup 64
Kebabs
    Fish 137
    Grilled Scallop 73
    Oyster 136
    Smoked Fish 74
Kedgeree 81
Kokada Salad 127

L

Leeks
    Fish and Leek Flan 84
    Fish Baked with Leeks and Corn 95
Lemon
    Flowers 149
    Ginger Fish 106
    Loops 148
    Oyster and Lemon Soup 62
    Twists 148
Light and Spicy Fish Curry 98

M

Marinara 105

Marinade Bacchus 76
Marinated
 Fish 126
 Fish Salad with Yoghurt
  Dressing 127
 Herb Marinated
  Mussels 76
 Seafood Platter 59
 Squid 129
 Summer Vegetable
  Marinated Fish 127
 Whole Fish for the
  Barbecue 135
Matsuo Squid 115
Mayonnaise 139
 Herb 139
 Pink 140
Mighty Mussel Salad 125
Mushroom Topping for Baked
 Fish 94
Mussels
 and Chive Salad 124
 and Squid in Basil
  Sauce 115
 Chowder 68
 Creamy Mussel Sauce for
  Pasta 117
 Crunchy Mussel
  Salad 120
 Herb Marinated 76
 How to Clean 36
 How to Cook 37
 How to Store 34
 in Wine 114
 Jiffy Mussel Chowder 63
 Mighty Mussel Salad 125
 Tasty Mussel Pie 83
 Toppings 56

N, O

Onion and Parsley Sauce 145
Open Crab Sandwiches 86
Oriental Fish Soup 60
Oysters
 and Lemon Soup 62
 and Spinach Crepes 73
 Fluffy Oyster Balls 53
 How to Cook 37
 How to Shuck 35
 How to Store 34
 Kebabs 136
 Kilpatrick 75
 Pâté 51
 Smoked Oyster
  Mousse 52
 Traditional Oyster and Veal
  Pie 112

P

Paella 109
Pain de Poisson 79

Parsley
 Dressing 129
 Onion and Parsley
  Sauce 145
 Sauce 144
Pâté
 Fish 51
 Oyster 51
 Parcels 52
 Pink and White
  Terrine 76
 Smoked Fish 51
Paua
 Devilled 113
 Steaks 113
Pasta
 Creamy Mussel Sauce for
  Pasta 117
 Pisces Pasta Dish 112
 Seafood and Pasta
  Soup 66
 Seafood, Feta Cheese and
  Pasta Salad 120
 Seafood Lasagne 104
 Smoked Fish and Pasta
  Salad 122
 Smoked Salmon and Caviar
  with Pasta 90
Pawpaw and Crab
 Entrée 71
Pies
 Fish and Asparagus
  Flan 84
 Fish and Celery Flan 84
 Fish and Leek Flan 84
 Fish and Spinach Flan 84
 Fisherman's Pie 110
 Tasty Mussel Pie 83
 Traditional Oyster and Veal
  Pie 112
Pink and White Terrine 76
Pink Mayonnaise 140
Piri Piri Sauce 145
Pisces Pasta Dish 112

Q, R

Refreshing Tuna Salad 123
Rice
 and Raisin Stuffing 134
 and Vegetable
  Stuffing 135
 Seafood Fried Rice 85
Roasted Shellfish 137
Rolled Fish Fillets with
 Vegetables 98

S

Salmon
 Loaf 80
 Salmon-Cheese Puff 82

Savoury Bake 89
Savoury Butter 141
Savoury Fish Casserole 111
Savoury Smoked Fish 88
Scallops
 and Fish Soup 69
 Cream-baked 75
 Grilled Scallop Kebabs 73
 How to Cook 37
 How to Open 36
 How to Store 34
Seafood
 and Pasta Soup 66
 Creamy Seafood Soup 67
 Crispy Seafood
  Surprises 55
 Dressing 122
 Feta Cheese and Pasta
  Salad 120
 Fried Rice 85
 Fritters 102
 Lasagne 104
 Marinated Seafood
  Platter 59
 Medley Soup 66
 Puff 82
 Stacked Seafood
  Crepes 72
 Stuffing 138
Seviche 70
Shellfish
 Cauldron 62
 Quiche 80
 Roasted 137
 Soup 66
Simple Fish Curry 97
Simple Smoked Salmon 58
Smoked Fish
 and Pasta Salad 122
 Cakes 102
 Cold-smoked Fish 33
 Hot-smoked Fish 33
 Kebabs 74
 Pâté 51
 Pilaf 103
 Roulade 86
 Salad 123
 Savoury Smoked Fish 88
Smoked Oyster Mousse 52
Smoked Salmon
 and Caviar with Pasta 90
 Loaf 80
 Simple Smoked
  Salmon 58
 Smoked Salmon-Cheese
  Puff 82
Smoked Seafood Platter 58
Sole or Flounder.
 Butterflied 138
Soused Fish 107
 Spicy Soused Fish 107
 Vegetable Soused
  Fish 108
Spiced Crab 114
Spiced Yoghurt Sauce 142

151

Spicy Cold Fish   106
Spicy Fish   78
Spicy Soused Fish   107
Spinach
   Fish and Spinach Flan   84
   Oyster and Spinach
      Crepes   73
Spring Onion Brush   147
Squid
   Baked Stuffed Squid   116
   Crumbed Squid Rings   70
   Marinated   129
   Matsuo   115
   Mussels and Squid in Basil
      Sauce   115
   Tropical Squid Salad   124
   with Black Bean
      Sauce   116
Stacked Seafood Crepes   72
Standard Crepe Recipe   72
Summer Vegetable Marinated
   Fish   127
Sweet and Sour Sauce   143

T

Tangy Herb Sauce   144
Taramasalata   54
Tarragon and Paprika
   Stuffing   134
Tartare Sauce   140
Tasty Mussel Pie   83
Tempura Batter for
   Seafood   118
Thousand Island
   Dressing   140
Tomato
   and Mushroom
      Stuffing   132
   Fresh Tomato Sauce   141
   or Lemon Flowers   149
   Stuffed with Smoked
      Oysters   56
Traditional Oyster and
   Veal Pie   112
Tropical Squid Salad   124

U, V, W

Vinaigrette Sauce   142
Vegetable Soused Fish   108
White Fish Stock   60
Whole Fish
   Barbecued   131
   Barbecued Stuffed   131
   Chinese-style   94
   Fried   100
   Marinated Whole Fish for
      the Barbecue   135
   with Tarragon   92
Wonderful Whisky-
   baked Fish   93

X, Y, Z

Yoghurt Garlic Dressing   120
Yoghurt Sauce, Spiced   142